Tactical Defensive Training for Real-Life Encounters

Tactical Defensive Training for Real-Life Encounters

Practical Self-Preservation for Law Enforcement

Paladin Press • Boulder, Colorado

Also by Ralph Mroz:

Defensive Shooting for Real-Life Encounters
Extreme Close-Quarters Shooting (video)

Tactical Defensive Training for Real-life Encounters:
Practical Self-Preservation for law Enforcement
by Ralph Mroz

Copyright © 2003 by Ralph Mroz

ISBN 13: 978-1-58160-427-6
Printed in the United States of America

Published by Paladin Press, a division of
Paladin Enterprises, Inc.
Gunbarrel Tech Center
7077 Winchester Circle
Boulder, Colorado 80301 USA
+1.303.443.7250

Direct inquiries and/or orders to the above address.

PALADIN, PALADIN PRESS, and the "horse head" design
are trademarks belonging to Paladin Enterprises and
registered in United States Patent and Trademark Office.

Visit our website at www.paladin-press.com

The purpose of firearms training is to prepare an officer to use firearms in a fight against an adversary in what usually begins as a spontaneous attack initiated by the adversary. Our firearms program is not about shooting. It is about fighting. When the concept of fighting is taken out of firearms training, we have forgotten the purpose of our training.

—*Lou Chiodo*

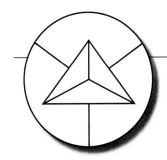

TABLE OF
CONTENTS

SECTION 1
SELF-DEFENSE IN CONTEXT

SECTION 2
SELF-DEFENSE SOFTWARE: THE MENTAL STUFF

SECTION 3
EDGED WEAPONS

SECTION 4
FIREARMS

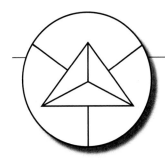

PREFACE

If anyone's to blame, it's probably Mike Boyle.

Back in the early '90s, I was attending an IALEFI (International Association of Law Enforcement Firearms Instructors) regional training conference that he was hosting. At that time he was already one of the top-dog writers at *Combat Handguns*. Having just published my first couple of articles, I introduced myself to Mike. In an offhand remark made while he was busy with the conference logistics, Mike said, "Keep writing—your opinion is just as valid as anyone's."

Well, I must have been genetically predisposed to have such a throwaway comment infect me, but that's all it took. Up until then I had thought that the couple of articles I had written had been a lark, and that that was that. (Certainly there's no money in writing.) But Mike's comment encouraged me to continue writing articles for the law-enforcement and self-defense press. As I did so, I realized not only that it was fun, but also that I was learning a lot. Being a "writer" gave me an excuse to call up experts in the field and pick their brains. And these experts were almost universally nice people who were happy to help me and the audience I was writing for to better understand some aspect of self-defense.

If I ever had any moments when I fancied myself an expert on a subject related to self-defense, that notion was quickly dispelled as I met an increasing number of *real* experts. I owe a debt of gratitude to all of these men and women who have helped and befriended me along this path. Some of them I talk with weekly, whereas I have exchanged only occasional e-mails with others. Since the distinction between those who have been more helpful to me than others is an arbitrary one, I will not attempt to list here all of the people to whom I owe acknowledgment. You know who you are; if we've ever had an intelligent conversation, or if you've ever shared a skill with me, thanks!

This book is a collection of my articles and columns that have appeared in several publications since my last Paladin Press book (*Defensive Shooting for Real-Life Encounters*) was written. The majority of these pieces appeared in either *Combat Handguns* or *Guns and Weapons for Law Enforcement* (both edited by Harry Kane), or *Tactical Knives* (another Harris Publications magazine, edited by Steven Dick). Both Harry and Steve know their stuff, and their support has been a high compliment to me.

Finally, although some of these pieces were written with a law enforcement audience in mind, their content applies equally to anyone.

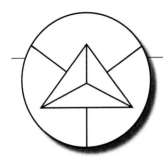

PHOTOGRAPH ACKNOWLEDGMENTS

Thanks to Mark Jacques and Ben Garvey for posing for the photographs in this book. Mark is a longtime friend, sounding board, and instructor. Ben is a new police officer who brings maturity and sensibility to the job.

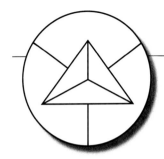

FOREWORD

BY YELENA PAWELA

A scholarly man once said, "As far as combatives go, only technologies change, methodologies do not."

From the Roman legions to the great armies of today, the factors that good soldiers, police officers, armed citizens, and other combatants rely on have remained constant: good weapons, good training, and good mental discipline.

However, every decade or so fresh thinkers, innovators of new ideologies, stir the pot with new approaches to combat. This, of course, upsets the "status quo."

However, for those for whom a regimented curriculum is ingrained, for people who are enslaved and bound to tradition and immortalized by legendary status in the world literature as experts, new ways if thinking about an old subject are held with contempt and disdain. Their line of thinking is, "How dare upstarts alter tradition faithfully passed down from generation to generation by venerated masters who tolerate only modest changes?"

Yet as times change, so must the way we train to fight. Sadly, so many lives have been lost unnecessarily because a general, administrator, or politician thought the best way to prepare his personnel to go into harm's way was to train the way he was trained back in the day. However, today soldier's tactics are not the same as they were a hundred years ago. Modern soldiers no more form line formations and shoot vollies against their enemies than today's police officers have to rely on Model 10 revolvers with dump pouches for spare ammunition. Times change, and so does our training.

Combatives is a thinking person's game. When revolutionaries like Bruce Lee stirred the pot in the '60s and '70s, going against traditionalists by cross-training in other "arts," it was not only unheard of but unmentionable. Today Jeet Kune Do (JKD) is one of the most advanced empty-hand combative forms on the planet.

In the '70s and '80s, revolutionaries like Massad Ayoob went against the teachers of the "new" pistolcraft and developed a shooting system that works under the most extreme cases of stress, appropriately called Stress Fire, which was adopted by the U.S. military and is now used by the thousands of trained military and law enforcement personnel alike.

Starting in the late '90s and continuing into the 21st century, another pundit of combatives has been stirring the pot. His name is Ralph Mroz. With his controversial and extremely effective approach to defensive shooting as described in *Defensive Shooting for Real-Life Encounters: A Critical Look at Current Training Methods* (Paladin Press, 2000), Ralph's approach of concentrating on empty-hand combatives to complement firearms in a critical situation is a subject that is long overdue.

Nothing is more important than survival training for those who need it the most, and those of us who know what it is like to survive confrontations owe our very lives to those who stir the pot. To the thinkers, those intellectuals who no longer accept yesterday's doctrines as gospel, we need all the scholarly literary pundits of combatives; we need more combative thinkers like Ralph Mroz, whose outlook on an old subject brings new thoughts that may one day save our very lives.

Yelena Pawela has trained in knife combatives with Russian and U.S. special forces instructors. She is formally trained in sambo and jujitsu and continues to study arnis, kali, eskrima, silat, and Jeet Kune Do. She has defended her life against a five-man assault after she was critically wounded in that attack with a knife. Yelena is a former police officer (Moscow, Russia) who worked with her department's narcotics and SWAT units as a K-9 officer. She holds a master's degree in animal behavior and is recognized as a top K-9 instructor. She is now the owner of Florida-based Counter Aggression Training Systems, where she teaches self-defense tactics with empty hands, knives, firearms, and K-9. She is on the staff of SWAT magazine and won a gold medal at the 2003 Arnold Schwarzenegger Martial Arts Classic.

Section 1

SELF-DEFENSE
IN CONTEXT

This section addresses the context of self-defense. Self-defense is but a piece of life—a means, not an end. By keeping it in perspective, we can ensure that the time we devote to it is consistent with our overall life goals.

Chapter 1

SELF-PRESERVATION:
THE BIGGER PICTURE

This book is about preserving your life and health in the face of forces that would harm them. My previous book in this vein, *Defensive Shooting for Real-Life Encounters* (Paladin Press, 2000), was mostly about training with firearms. This book goes a bit further afield, addressing both the hardware and the software that you need to survive. Chapter 2 places self-defense in the context of the hardware and software skills necessary for it, and the remaining chapters address specific points regarding them. Many of these chapters originally appeared as columns or articles in various magazines, and thus they represent a sprinkling of my thinking on the subject. This chapter, however, addresses the context of weapon-based self-defense in general.

WHAT THREATENS YOU?

Referring to the first sentence above, the logical question to ask is, "What are the forces that are out there trying to harm you?" Yes, there are criminals of all manner who prey on law-abiding people, and they usually come to mind when the subject of self-defense comes up. Yet they are the least of your worries. Criminals can't really rob you of your life or health anyway—time and God will take both away eventually. What they *can* do is shorten the time in which you enjoy that life and health. That's an important distinction to keep in mind. It's preserving *extra time* in life or health that is our self-defense goal—not preserving life and health itself.

Why is this important? Because logically we ought to first address those enemies that are most likely to rob us of that extra time. And criminals don't top the list—disease and accidents do. Therefore, our self-defense efforts need to start with maintaining our health and observing commonsense safety procedures. Weapons come later, if we want to be rational.

THE FIVE PILLARS OF HEALTH

It has always amused me to see weapons instructors smoking cigarettes. I mean, here they are spending all this time and energy training to survive a gunfight, which is a very unlikely occurrence. Yet they go to great expense and spend a considerable amount of time in the deliberate act of cutting their lives short . . . through the avenue of a very painful death, to boot. Of course they have a right to do so. But it makes no sense whatsoever. It is irrational.

Likewise with fitness and health. Most people who study weapons for self-defense would reap a far greater health and longevity return on their time if they spent their range time at the gym, or running, or engaging in some form of exercise. A fat person who carries a gun for self-defense is a walking contradiction. It is irrational.

Our ancestors didn't have to worry about staying in shape. When they weren't dying of disease or in war, they were working their butts off. Today, even with our sedentary lives, staying in shape is no great mystery—the five components are well known and easy to do.

Staying healthy is the first task of those who want to prolong their lives. The author does squats as part of his weekly regimen.

Aerobic conditioning is simple: simply exert 70 percent of your maximum heart rate (which is 220 minus your age) for 20 minutes three times a week. Run, ski, whatever. Just get the heart pumping. Muscle tone is accomplished through *resistance exercise*. That's weights and/or weight machines. Weights aren't just for young people, either. The studies are now proving what many smart elders have long known, and that's that weight training has great benefits even for elderly people. Join a gym or buy a set of weights, get some sound advice on their use (which is plentiful), and pump iron three times a week. *Flexibility* is critical for maintaining range of motion. There are many good books on stretching, and there are even stretching classes at most gyms. Five minutes a day with a good regimen will work wonders.

Stress management is finally getting its due as a health pre-server. The frenetic pace of our lives and the demands of a society in which we live to do more and accomplish more are not what Mother Nature had in mind when she designed our nervous systems. We now know that an awful lot of people live most of their lives in a mild or medium state of inappropriate sympathetic nervous system activation. In plain English, they are walking around in a state of fight-or-flight arousal most of the day. Hypertension, heart disease, ulcers, fatigue—the list of ailments caused by undue stress goes on and on. Managing stress is thus a critical component of modern life, and exercise can play a double role here because it is often a good stress reliever. Ingesting drugs—including alcohol—is *not* a good way to manage stress. Drugs of any sort are bad for you mentally, spiritually, and physically. Putting that beer down and going for a run will not only spare you the damage caused by alcohol, it will also blow off some stress and keep you in shape.

Finally, *diet* is a critical piece of your strategy for warding off bad health or premature death. Eating "clean," as the athletes refer to it, is necessary. Once you do, eating bad doesn't feel good, so it's a self-reinforcing practice. Not eating the bad stuff is the easy part to understand. Chips, soda, too much fat, sugar, artificial goop, trans-fats (hydrogenated oils), and so on—we all know we should mostly avoid (though not necessarily completely eschew) these. It gets trickier, though, when we get into managing our macronutrients (protein, carbohydrates, and fat) and micronutrients (vitamins, herbs, and minerals). Nutrition isn't my area of professional expertise, but I can offer a few helpful hints. In terms of macronutrient composition, it is becoming increasingly apparent that the high-carbohydrate diet advocated by the government for the last 20 years is wrong. Protein is vital, and more and more studies indicate that something like a "Zone" diet (30 percent of your calories from protein, 30 percent from fat, and 40 percent from carbohydrates; sometimes referred to as a "40/30/30" diet) is the healthiest—or, at the very least, is a good, healthy approach. One possible reason a carbohydrate-heavy diet has become detrimental to our health today whereas so many earlier peoples seem to have done so well on this type of diet is that the grains that compose the bulk of carbohydrates today have been drastically altered by selective breeding for increased crop yield over the last 70 years. The wheat that your great-grandfather ate contained several times as much protein as the wheat that you are likely to buy today.

When it comes to micronutrients, it takes a lot of hours to sort through all the claims, and the "right" path isn't clear. My advice is to read as much as you have the interest to, and then seek the advice of those in your community who do follow this area closely—and follow it. Just doing this will put you ahead of most. One thing is certain, though—you will have to supplement your diet to achieve optimum health. Nature is done with us as soon as we've raised our children to childbearing age, and up through the 19th century, a man over 40 was old. Modern medicine has contrived to extend Mother Nature's planned demise for us, and our part of the bargain is that we have to compensate with appropriate nutrients to keep us running at ages that she never intended us to reach.

You can't ignore diet. The longest-lived people in the world (as long as there have been records) have always eaten a diet very different from the traditional Western diet that most of us consume today. It is literally and obviously true: you are what you eat. Yet somehow, the complete obviousness of this statement has led to most people's not seeing it! Bottom line: if prolonging your life is the objective, then you need to seriously consider your eating patterns.

COMMONSENSE SAFTY

How many folks who keep a gun in the house for self-defense don't have a fire extinguisher there? How many don't wear their seat belts? How many don't know CPR and basic First Responder skills? This is a short section because there isn't much to say that's not obvious. You're much more likely to have to use CPR to help a loved one than to have to use your gun to help one. Just follow the logic and invest in the safety measures that are most likely to be of need.

Knowing CPR is far more likely to save a loved one than employing a firearm. How many readers are qualified?

Preserving Our Lives and Our Health

So, if preserving your life and health, if buying time to enjoy them more, is your objective, then you can see that the gun, the knife, and empty-hand self-defense skills are well down the list of things we ought to invest our limited time and energy in.

I will assume that you, the reader, have already made these prior investments, and that the next most useful expenditure of your time is in the traditional self-defense skills.

Because that's what this book is about.

Chapter 2

PHYSICAL SELF-DEFENSE IN CONTEXT

Talk self-defense and people think of knives, guns, or martial arts—whichever is their favorite. That's a hardware perspective (I realize that calling martial arts skills "hardware" is a bit of a semantic stretch), and it's right as far as it goes. But there are the software components of self-defense, too, and they are even more important. The following diagram depicts the hardware and software elements of self-defense together.

The triangle at the center represents the three basic hardware competencies that are necessary in self-defense: *empty-hand* skills (tan), *contact weapon* (knife, stick) skills (silver), and *distance weapon* (primarily firearms) skills (black). The larger trisected circle that surrounds the triangle represents the software context in which the hardware is used. The three elements of the software context are the *will* (red) to defend yourself, the *skill* (blue) with which to do it, and the *awareness* (yellow) to allow you to do it. The idea that these elements come together is hardly original; people have been saying similar things for

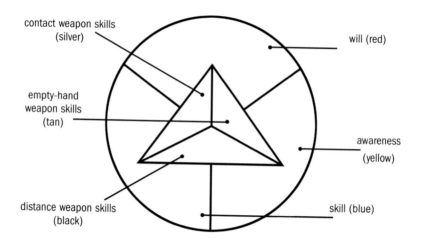

contact weapon skills (silver)

will (red)

empty-hand weapon skills (tan)

awareness (yellow)

distance weapon skills (black)

skill (blue)

thousands of years. But this particular ordering of the elements is the way I find it most useful to view the entire self-defense context in the 21st century.

Empty-hand skills are certainly the foundation of any self-defense curriculum. Even those who focus on weapons as a means of self-defense rely on foundational empty-hand skills as the basis for their weapons skills. Balance, power, stability, timing, coordination, and kinesthetic development are necessary for any sort of actual self-defense—whether you're shooting a gun, deploying a knife, or evading and punching. That's why weapons skills are always enhanced by the development of good empty-hand skills and why martial artists seem to make the transition to the gun better than gunners tend to pick up empty-hand combative skills, in my experience.

Even if you tend to regard a weapon of some sort as your primary self-defense option, remember that attacks often come spontaneously and without warning—out of the blue. And they come close-up. The brutal truth is that you will have to deal with any such attack first with empty hands—and then access your weapon if time allows. There will simply be no time to draw a weapon that's not already in hand in these cases. For

Empty-hand skills are even more necessary than firearms skills. Here world-class instructor Andy Stanford demonstrates a point to a class with Claude Werner.

this reason alone, sheer logic dictates that of all the self-defense skills to acquire, empty-hand skills are primary and should be learned first. The question of which particular empty-hand skills is beyond the scope of this discussion, but let me just suggest that good old Western boxing is a superlative place to begin. Boxing is one of the cornerstones of most practical self-defense systems, and its instruction is widely available. Also, boxers actually hit each other, and you've got to get used to getting hit in your training. The first time you feel the pain and disorientation of a good head shot should *not* be on the street when someone's trying to kill you.

Contact weapon skills are also necessary. Sometimes you need more help than empty hands can provide, and contact weapons skills are simply a good way to up the odds in your favor. Sticks (canes), pepper spray (OC), and knives are the most common contact weapons used.

Walking sticks are legal everywhere and don't get a second glance. They are already in your hand and are thus fast into action. Good stick instruction is becoming more and more widely available, and what's generally regarded as the ultimate stick art, Filipino arnis (aka escrima), is very common these days. Arnis is a heck of a lot of fun to learn, to boot, and it's eminently suitable for anyone of any age because it requires more grace than physical effort. And if you can handle a walking stick, you can wield anything that resembles one, such as an umbrella or piece of lumber—whatever's handy.

Pepper spray is also widely available now, and no one should be without it. It does not work with 100 percent effectiveness all the time (or even at all some of the time), but generally it is very effective and works wonders. It also works on dogs quite well; I've used it several times on dogs that were trying to bite me as I ran. It's also extremely safe and does no damage to either attacker or victim. Although it would seem that using a can of "criminal spray-away" would be simplicity itself, it is well worth your while to take a proper course in its use from a certified instructor. There's just a lot of stuff that you will learn that will be helpful, not the least of which is what kind of pepper spray to buy. There are at least three main spray variants as of this writing (stream, mist, and fog), many concentrations of the active substance, and several carrier formulations. It really is quite important to get the right product for your anticipated use. Finally, don't neglect to take the opportunity in class to get sprayed yourself. This is a must! Because when you spray someone else, it's a pretty sure bet that you will receive some of your own discharged medicine. You need to know how to handle this and not be surprised and shocked by it (that's what should happen to your assailant).

Knives are lethal-force contact weapons. As such, the same restrictions are placed on their use (legally and morally) as firearms. Yes, it's been said that "you can cut someone a little, but you can't shoot him a little." I suppose that this is just as true as saying that you can use a gun to either "wing" someone or kill him. Both statements are theoretically true, but in practice—in the messy, unpredictable dynamics of violent encounters—controlling the damage that an inherently lethal weapon produces is unlikely. Don't count on it. And certainly any court in this land will judge you to have used lethal force whenever you employ either of these weapons, whatever your intent or the actual damage. The good news is that knives are widely available and that a practical self-defense knife of some sort is legal almost everywhere in the United States (the same can't be said for some other countries). More good news: we are in the golden age of defensive knife production. Unbelievably excellent self-defense knives—in design, in materials, and in manufacture—are available everywhere now at very competitive prices. Using a knife is simplicity itself, and again, the Filipino arts are generally regarded as elegantly simple and exquisitely effective. (Other knife systems are also effective, of course.) A knife isn't quite as versatile or effective as a gun in many self-defense situations, but when you can't carry a gun, a knife hardly leaves you unarmed.

Distance weapons—we're talking guns here. There's so much good advice available in magazines and books and from scores of excellent instructors that I don't need to say much here except to make sure that you avail yourself of them. I make the assumption here that all readers are familiar with either these sources or the material already. My main point is that distance weapons (guns) are but one of three hardware elements that you need to have to protect yourself and those for whom you're responsible. They should not be your only focus or area of competence.

More good news, though: we're also in a golden age of firearms manufacture and firearms instruction. There are more excellent guns made now than ever before in history, and the level of professional instruction available is the most practical and effective that it's ever been. How long this will last, I have no idea—so get the training you need ASAP!

Awareness is the primary software skill that you need. It's the *sine qua non* of self-defense—the "necessary and sometime sufficient" skill that is required. Without awareness of an existing or impending situation, you are left to react rather than act; you are guaranteed to be behind the power curve from the get-go. You will be starting at least 1/4 second behind your opponent, and even that slight gap can be decisive. That 1/4 second is only theoretical, however, as it relates only to the reaction time of a well-practiced young individual. Factor in the fact that most of us aren't in the same state of mental and physical condition as a 24-year-old SPECWAR operator, and that we will also have to recover from being startled, and there's probably an easy full-second advantage to the bad guy if you are taken by surprise. And an entire second is as long as many fights last. Without awareness you have nothing—you are a victim waiting to happen. With it, you can avoid having to fight at all in many cases.

Awareness is a state of mind. It is an inculcated skill that can be learned. Like all skills, it is perishable. As the very foundation of your survival, it deserves primary attention. Practice requires nothing more than a commitment to remaining aware for increasing periods of time, and anyone at all can master it. What makes it so simple is that it is simply a matter of wanting to do it and devoting time to it . . . which is what makes it so hard. You can't run down to your local dealer and purchase it.

Will—as in being willing to do what's necessary to preserve your life—is the next necessary skill. Massad Ayoob refers to this as "*the question.*" The question he's alluding to is, "Will I take another human life if need be?" You had better know *for sure* the answer to this Mother of All Questions. You need to answer it intellectually, emotionally, and spiritually. You need to examine the question calmly in light of your beliefs, investigate your emotional responses through realistic training, and come to terms with the moral implications of taking someone's life in self-defense.

For some this is a trivially easy exercise; for some it is gut-wrenching. You can't purchase these answers, either.

Skill is required to effectively employ whatever weapon you use (empty hand, contact, or distance). It's not enough to have a gun or knife or to know some martial arts techniques. You must spend time to develop the skill necessary to employ these weapons under the fast, chaotic, messy, and violent dynamics of a real fight for your life. You need not devote your entire life to their development, but there's no way around the fact that time is definitely required. Nothing worth having is free, after all, and time is our most valuable commodity!

You will shorten considerably the time required to acquire sufficient skill by choosing your training curriculum wisely. Traditional martial arts certainly have self-defense value, but that's not their exclusive or even main goal. Studying a system devoted entirely to realistic empty-hand defense will get you to competence in this area faster. Likewise with contact and distance weapons. For example, some of the skills necessary for pistol-based self-defense will be developed by competitive shooting. But a considerably faster way to acquire an acceptable level of firearms survival competence is to focus your training entirely on self-defense shooting, especially through the use of realistic simulations equipment such as Simunitions or AirSoft.

Empty-hand weapons, contact weapons, and firearms; awareness, will, and skill. These are the six elements of self-defense. They interact with and support each other, and you need them all!

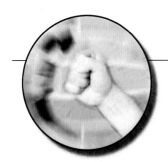

Chapter 3

SELF-DEFENSE HARDWARE

Although we have been disavowed of the notion that man's uniqueness is his ability to use tools, our ability to complexly fashion them is certainly a unique capability within the animal kingdom. From the simple flashlight to pinpoint, laser-guided bombs, the range of tools that we have at our disposal for self-defense is awesome and their capabilities are impressive.

Personal self-defense tools are no exception to this rule. Countless magazines, books, videos, and seminars are devoted to the understanding and use of personal defense tools. Naturally, if we were to carry a version of every useful tool out there, we'd quickly run out of pockets and belt space, so we have to be selective. Choosing our armory of personal defense tools intelligently is dependent on our understanding of the different modes of self-defense, their place in the force continuum, and their relationship to each other—and then choosing a set of tools that matches our capabilities and situation. Choosing a self-defense armory is no more a matter of

You won't find competent professionals without a white light source. Here a Surefire light rests next to a spare magazine.

just strapping on a quatro-cinco than it is loading up on "one of everything."

THE FORCE CONTINUUM

The *force continuum* is a well-established concept in police work, as well as in *responsible* non-law-enforcement curricula. The essential concept here is that there are differing levels of force that you can be confronted with, and that the level constrains the amount of force with which you can respond. Most readers will be familiar with this concept, and the main implication of it in terms of our personal armory is that we need to have the ability to respond to all levels of threat with an appropriate weapon. Just what that weapon is for any particular threat will vary from person to person. Bruce Lee, if he were still alive, may need nothing more than his empty hands for even threats involving lethal weapons. On the other hand, little

Competence at delivering verbal commands is foundational in self-defense. Here Andy Stanford role-plays in a scenario with writer Anthony Lombardo.

ol' Granny may well need a gun for dealing with something that you or I could handle with our bare hands.

AN INTELLIGENT ARMORY

Essentially, the intelligently armed person will be capable of responding with six levels of force: verbal commands, white light, pepper spray, empty-hand techniques, impact weapons, and lethal force. This does not necessarily imply, however, that one must carry six weapons.

Verbal commands are a police officer's mainstay, and wonderful results can come from using them. The trick is to 1) actually be prepared to back them up if necessary, and 2) sound like you can back them up. Most people are simply not used to commanding others in a direct, forceful manner. It takes most police recruits some time before they are comfortable doing so and doing so reflexively. So you'll have to practice in force-on-force simulations if you're not a police officer. "DON'T MOVE"; "DON'T MAKE ME SHOOT YOU"; "SHOW ME YOUR HANDS"; "DON'T COME ANY CLOSER." These and other appropriate commands need to be practiced and made reflexive when necessary. Once that's accomplished, this "weapon" of countermanding force will always be with you.

White light is now available in such small packages and with such blinding power (measured in *lumens*) that it can be considered a force option in itself. Surefire is certainly the leader in this field, and rare is the true professional who does not always have a Surefire light with him or her. Merely shining one of these lights in an assailant's eyes will temporarily disable him. And if you need to use a higher force level, using white light in conjunction with it is a force multiplier. All this, in addition to the light's initial self-justifying potential as an illumination source! Best yet, white light is not even considered force by the courts, yet it functions just like it.

Pepper spray (OC) is next up on the force level. This spray disables many aggressive people much of the time, and is safer to employ (for both you and your assailant) than mixing it up with strikes. OC is essentially at the same level as "soft" hands techniques like locks and holds, but *much* easier to employ and therefore preferable (joint locks and holds are all but impossible to achieve in real life). As a rule, you can use it whenever you feel that you are about to be or are being touched unlawfully. OC is an invaluable tool and is another item that few professionals are often without.

Empty-hand techniques—and here I mean "hard" techniques, or strikes—are sometimes called for, yet no higher level of force is. When you're in that situation, you need them, and nothing else will do. So empty-hand competence is another "weapon" that no professional is without. But more importantly, empty-hand skills are the foundation for competence at all force levels, from verbal commands to firearms. By training in them you achieve balance, coordination, inoculation to the effects of stress, a reflexive attack response, and a warrior spirit—all of which are essential to using any weapon. These are absolutely crucial.

Impact weapons are between hard empty-hand techniques and lethal weapons on the force continuum, and they are very useful when appropriate. But hard strikes can be substituted for impact weapons, and doing so means one less weapon to tote about. Some professionals do choose to carry an impact weapon (e.g., a collapsible baton or a cane) to fill the small gap between hard strikes and lethal weapons, and some don't.

Lethal-force options usually mean a firearm or a knife. And make no mistake about it—a knife is a lethal-force tool, both in practice and in the eyes of the law. It differs from the pistol (for non-law-enforcement applications) mostly in its lack of distance advantage. Either way, you have the ultimate option should it be necessary and justified.

Notice that I have not included some things in this list of tools for covering the spectrum of the six force-level responses. "Novelty" items like saps, brass knuckles (even if made of plastic), Kubutons or their ilk, and so on are not included for two reasons: 1) they are mostly gimmicks, often not effective in real life at all, and 2) they do not efficiently cover a significant part of the force continuum spectrum. They are just so much junk to fill your already full pockets with.

You Can Have It All

The six levels of force discussed above can be covered with but three weapons: a good light, a can of OC, and a gun or knife. Armed with these, plus the ever-present verbal-command capability and empty-hand skills, you are about as prepared as you can practically be to get through almost any conceivable scenario. And they are not so much of a collective load so as to be impracticable or even uncomfortable. When you're wearing a coat, they demand only a holster and a pocket or two. In hot weather they can be carried comfortably in a belly pack. Of course, you'll need good software skills (awareness, mind-set, and so on) to accompany this hardware, good training with these weapons, and force-on-force practice. But your basic hardware kit is really pretty simple.

Remember, Murphy is alive. The tool you choose not to carry will almost certainly be the one you need!

Section 2

Self-Defense Software:
The Mental Stuff

This section is mostly concerned with the software elements of self-defense discussed earlier: will, skill, and awareness. These tend to get short shrift in the self-defense literature, but they are foundational. Without them, no hardware matters. Yet they are elusive and difficult to teach. If someone wants to make a truly useful mark on self-defense training—and do mankind a lot of good, too—he or she should concentrate here and figure out how to effectively transmit these qualities.

Chapter 4

ALERT OR ASLEEP?
WHY SOME PEOPLE SEE DANGER COMING AND SOME DON'T

All trainers teach their students what the danger signals are—an assailant's body language or unnatural attention, being followed, and so on. Every trainer also gives the requisite lecture on "staying in Condition Yellow." Yet when the threat is real, only some students will pick up on danger cues while others will wind up in the hospital. Why? Why are some people oblivious and some vigilant? What's the key to being alert . . . and not asleep?

Having wondered about this for 25 years, and having never arrived at a satisfactory answer, I decided to poll some real experts.

Mike Conti, a well-known writer and trainer, is now in charge of the Massachusetts State Police firearms program:

> I've come to believe that regardless of training exposure, some people simply "have it" and some don't. Of

those who "have it," some have a lot and some don't. While training can help, I've come to believe that some just don't have it in them to a degree that they can effectively operate in extreme conditions on an ongoing basis.

I've worked with officers with eyes and officers who literally didn't see a knife in the hand of a person they had pinned to a wall. I've seen people pick up a signal from an individual, make a good investigative stop, and find that this was indeed a real bad guy, while others would talk to this same person and remark that he "seemed like a nice guy."

Personally, I believe it's the predatory instinct. Some people are simply better hunters than others. When you take someone who has been born with a combination of natural hunter's instincts, a fair level of intelligence, and an ability to learn and apply lessons in a commonsense manner, you've got all the makings of an excellent hunter.

Lou Chiodo, former USMC captain and one of the new generation of star firearms instructors:

It all has to begin with discussion of situation awareness. This is a starting point in what should be a continual training process—yet unfortunately, it is where many training programs end. This effort results in merely education—not training. Once we have discussed the issue in the classroom, the *education* has to be turned into *training* by putting an individual through controlled drills that allow him to feel and experience the need for situational awareness.

As martial artists, we both know that real-time, real-speed training is necessary to become fully aware of how any technique will work. A necessary step in developing situational awareness is to subject [students] to a wide range of problems and let them experience how important it is to pay attention to the environment.

Controlled force-on-force drills using Airsoft pistols is a necessary component of realistic training. Note the yellow markings on the pistols denoting them as nonlethal weapon replicas.

I talk to every trainee about how really fast things happen in the field. No matter how much we discuss it, it never really hits home until something happens in a real-world encounter. Some people, however, seem to have a hard time maintaining concentration and awareness, and these may be the people that need to find another line of work. Some people are just not cut out for certain jobs.

Bert DuVernay is the former director of the Smith & Wesson Academy, a police chief, and one of the finest thinkers in the business:

I think that modern approaches to simulation training help, but I don't know of any data on the subject. I think the key to learning to stay in yellow, and to recognizing danger signs, is *motivation*—just like learning anything else.

Some people become motivated because they've been victimized; some out of professionalism as they assume a warrior's life. If [people are] truly motivated, if they have access to current information and/or training methods, if they have some feedback concerning their performance, then they should learn.

As far as how to [instill recognition of] the "setup" of an attack or a crime, I'm afraid I don't know. It may be the difference between being a meat-eater and a grass-eater. How can a grass-eater hunt a meat-eater? On the other hand, in the animal world, the grass-eaters are quite adept at avoiding the meat-eaters. Perhaps the difference is that animals don't (to our knowledge) engage in denial, while humans certainly do.

Another disadvantage of human grass-eaters is embarrassment. It is known that victims will recognize a situation that causes all their instincts to cry out and identify as dangerous, but, since they don't want to appear rude or, in some cases, racially prejudiced, continue on that course of action that leads them to be victimized.

Ed Lovette and Dave Spaulding, both recognizable authors and trainers, have written a book titled *Defensive Living* (Looseleaf Law Publications, 2002). In it they note that people who score high as conceptualizers on the Meyers-Briggs personality test seem to have trouble noticing the details of life around them. "To simply tell these folks to be aware of their environment is not good enough. You must also *show* them."

Well-known writer Kelly McCann (aka "Jim Grover"), a man who has spent a lot of time himself in hostile environments all around the globe, notes in his book *Street Smarts, Firearms, and Personal Security* (available from Paladin Press), "Many people engage in negative reinforcement . . . when they suspect something is about to happen, they think, 'Oh, it's probably nothing.'"

Clyde Caceres is an accomplished martial artist and

firearms trainer. He is probably the world's leading authority on the tactical use of laser sights on handguns:

> Though certain people may be genetically imprinted with a Condition-Yellow mind-set, my experiences working with people who maintain a vigilant state of alertness indicate that it's important how one perceives danger.
>
> A perception of danger may have been instilled through exposure to stimuli of harm. I have taught many people who seem to believe that, "If I ignore danger, it won't happen." But when having been confronted by an incident—one that may range from a brush with danger to having received physical harm—the often-found new response is, "Never again." It's unfortunate that the word "again" has to be associated with the newfound respect for harm, but . . .
>
> Some people have an *academic* development of heightened awareness. I believe they respond to incidents they have been exposed to, even if the harm was not directed at them. They come up with a cognitive thought process that says, "it happened to them," "it happened near me," "it happened in a circumstance similar to what I exist in," and so on; "I want to learn not to let it happen to me." Some people have a *learned* development of heightened awareness, perhaps through military training, hunting, paint ball, competition, etc.
>
> Some people have a sense of self-worth, and others succumb. Some people anticipate the potential for others to do bad, and some naively assume others [have] only good intentions. It sort of boils down to what you want to believe vs. what is reality.

John Farnam needs no introduction to established self-defense students. To the new ones, let me just say that John is one of the most respected people in the business.

I have always found that, without the requiem philosophical overlay, merely teaching people a series of psychomotor skills does little to enhance their survivability. To most of the "grass-eater" people, victimization, like cancer, is something that will probably get us all at some point. They resist thinking about it because they don't want to go through the disciplined drudgery of self-improvement. As trainers, we therefore must spoon-feed them the hard, lumpy, bad-tasting medicine of truth.

Walt Rauch, a familiar name, has lived a fair amount of his life in hostile environments and in a mental state somewhat beyond yellow. His remarks are trenchant and brief: "People live in Condition White because they want to. People live in Condition Yellow because they want to. I live aware because I accept the world as it is—not as I want it to be."

So the factors that cause a person to recognize danger signals represent a mixture of nature, nurture, and self-direction. The five factors mentioned repeatedly by our experts are genetics, realistic training (or life experience), motivation, a realistic acceptance of the world (lack of denial), and discipline. Common sense would dictate that a severe deficiency of genetics would not be compensated for by an abundance of training, and that lack of training would hamper even a genetically predisposed person. But what to say of those factors that must come from within: motivation, a realistic outlook, and discipline? Are these also genetic? Can they be instilled?
Wish I knew.

Chapter 5

SEEING IT COMING

It amazes me how many people seem to think that the gun they carry legally is some sort of talisman that wards off evil. They religiously strap on their gun (and, if they're smart, some spare ammunition, a flashlight, and a canister of pepper spray), yet they go about their business in perpetual Condition White (unaware of their surroundings).

Maybe they just don't know how to be street-smart.

Since I live in a relatively peaceful corner of the world, I asked David James, the head honcho at the Vee-Arnis-Jitsu School of Self-Defense in New York City, what he teaches his students about being street-smart. (Shihan James' school ranks with the best in street-realistic schools, and it's certainly where I'd be working out if I lived in NYC.) Here's his advice:

> First, stay aware of your surroundings. Go about in Condition Yellow. (Condition Yellow is a state of relaxed awareness.) This is fundamental. Most successful street

The correct way to give a stranger the time: lift the watch to your face so that he remains in your field of vision.

assaults are the result of the victim's being surprised by the attack. Simply being aware of a potential assailant is enough to make his job more difficult. Remember—attackers don't come out of thin air. You'll see the signs if you're mindful. Watch out for people focusing on you. Most people don't stare or look for long periods at other people. If someone, or a group of people, is watching you for too long, something's not right.

If someone asks you for something—anything—be wary. Either don't answer, or answer tactically. For example, give the time with your wrist in front of your face, not looking down, where you can't be aware of what's happening. For the same reason, watch out for someone handing you a piece of paper with an address on it and asking for directions. Don't look down at it. Instead, take it from the person's hand and hold it up to your eyes to read it.

Decline to give "spare change" politely—and beware of panhandlers who don't take "no" for an answer—they could want more than your spare change.

If someone stops you, make sure you're not surrounded by his or her buddies—and put your back to a parked car or a building to avoid being blindsided.

If you think you're being followed or you're approached by a suspicious person or people, you can cross the street. If they do, too, that's a giveaway. If you know you're being targeted, you have several options. You can walk in the middle of the street—it draws attention to you, which is the last thing your potential attackers want. You can turn around suddenly and walk back toward the potential assailants who are following you. (Yes, this puts you closer to them, but it also surprises them and throws them off guard. Furthermore, if you were where they wanted to assault you, they'd have done so. So take advantage of the fact that where you are now isn't where they wanted to commit the crime.) You can stop and put your back to a parked car or building. Let them confront you frontally—if they are going to at all—in the place you choose, rather than sneak up from behind.

Avoidance is always the best course. Stay out of unsafe areas or any area in which you feel uncomfortable. Leave any area where you suddenly get a bad feeling. Trust your instincts. All of this is obvious, and you've heard it before. But it's astounding just how many victims ignore their feelings and common sense. Make a resolution to act on this knowledge. Learning by mistakes is a lousy way to learn!

In the same vein, don't get into an elevator with persons you're uncomfortable with. Just snap your fingers, say, "Damn, I forgot something," and leave. Give suspicious persons a wide berth. If they then crowd you, something's awry.

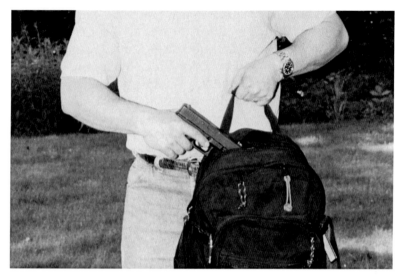

Drawing a weapon from an off-body carrier requires practice—both to understand the extra time required and to make it smooth.

If you feel you're being watched, followed, or pursued, put your hand in your pocket conspicuously. You probably should be carrying some sort of weapon there anyway, which is good—now you're prepared. Even if you're not, it will look like you are. Violent criminals are lazy, and an armed, prepared, alert victim is not what they're looking for.

Make sure you carry your protective weapon(s) in an easy-to-access place. If your gun is on your hip, keep your coat unbuttoned. If you carry your gun in a difficult-to-access place, like a case or purse, you owe it to yourself to run through some real-life scenarios to see just how far behind the curve this puts you—sometimes too far. If you carry in these places, be very aware of the extra risk you take; guns are not good-luck charms! Make sure you know how to employ your weapons at close range under severe time constraints and acting in response to an assault cue. Most of the commonly taught methods for employing a handgun in close quarters simply don't work (see my video, *Extreme Close Quarters Shooting*, from Paladin Press to verify this). The fact is that you won't always be able to get to that gun you count on for self-defense. The fact is that in real life, you need to know both armed and unarmed self-defense methods. Which of them you get to employ will be determined by your attacker, not you.

Finally, if you don't live in New York, let me recommend David James' videotapes. Information on them is available at the Vee-Arnis-Jitsu Web site (www.veearnisjitsu.com).

Chapter 6

THE COLOR CODES–AGAIN (BUT RIGHT)

THE COLOR CODES

Most readers are familiar with the color code system for categorizing awareness and combat states. The color code system is a great tool, and one that we can all use to further our own cause or in teaching others. But there seem to be several

White	Yellow	Orange	Red	Black
Oblivious to surroundings	Relaxed awareness	Aware of something (potentially) wrong	Identification of what's wrong and reacting to it appropriately	Combat

versions of it floating around, and every time I read about them, the system changes. Let me present the system here as I think it best fits civilian self-defense.

This is the way the color codes were presented to me by Massad Ayoob when I took his famous LFI-1 course many years ago. Mas explained that a similar color code had existed in the military, except that red and black were combined, because in war you engage the enemy upon sight (generally). For civilian use (both law enforcement and non-law enforcement), the five stages make more sense. Here's why and what they mean:

White

Condition White is being completely unaware of your surroundings. You're in Condition White if you're walking down the street and you come up on someone (or someone comes up on you) without your being aware of that person's presence prior to the encounter. This is the normal state of most people most of the time! Most people have no idea what's going on around them—that's why they make such easy victims. It's an easy state to slip into, and we've all done it by daydreaming, being preoccupied with some thought, or whatever. Of course, when we're reading or concentrating on some activity, we're in Condition White as far as our surroundings go . . . at least temporarily. We can, however, train ourselves to break out of White periodically in these circumstances. It goes without saying that in Condition White, we are at a severe disadvantage as far as self-defense goes.

Yellow

Condition Yellow is a state of relaxed awareness. Here our blood pressure remains normal and we remain relaxed, all the while taking in our surroundings. We are in Condition Yellow when we're driving a car and paying attention to the driving. Col. Jeff Cooper noted that a person can spend every waking hour in Condition Yellow and suffer no ill effects. It does, however, take considerable training and discipline to maintain this state. The natural tendency is to slip into White. In Yellow you should generally pick up on warning signs of danger, and this is the state you should strive to be in as much as possible.

Orange

Condition Orange is that state when "something seems wrong." Perhaps you've noticed that three young males have just split up ahead of you. Maybe you've realized that the car behind you has been there too long. You might have noticed that the house doesn't seem quite the way you left it. Something might be wrong, or something is wrong but you don't know exactly what it is yet. Orange is when arousal sets in, and at this point you should begin to act cautiously and with a deliberate plan of action.

Red

In Condition Red you've identified that something is wrong and you know what it is. The three thugs are making an obvious attempt to encircle you; the car is definitely following you; someone has broken into your house. Here you initiate your self-defense program. You may move to cover, take evasive action, issue verbal commands, perhaps even present a weapon—whatever the appropriate tactics are. These are the situations for which you spend most of your time training; this is where your tactics and skill come into play. If you are effective with your tactics here, you can often stop the assault. That would be ideal because the only other option is to enter Condition Black.

Black

Condition Black is actual combat. It is preferable not to go here, but sometimes it's inevitable. Here your skill at arms will be the deciding factor.

You can see here why Conditions Red and Black differ, and why the distinction is important for civilian use. Knowing that the stages of a fight are measured in fractions of a second, it's clear that being surprised by an assault is a potentially decisive negative factor in the fight's outcome. This is why all good teachers harp on staying in Condition Yellow. So avoiding the fight, or seeing it coming if it's inevitable, is at least as important as honing your skills for the fight itself. Yet how much time do you spend training in *these skills* compared to the time you spend on your fighting skills?

THE OODA LOOP

Better thinkers than I have identified the fact that all hostile engagements are a competition for time. Col. John Boyd's famous OODA Loop paradigm is perhaps the most elegant practical refinement of this basic insight. OODA stands for Observe, Orient, Decide, and Act. These are the basic actions that you must take in a fight—any fight. You must first observe (become aware of) a threat or opportunity, then orient yourself to it, then decide what to do about it, and then act on that decision. Your adversary is doing the same thing, of course. The person who can move through the OODA Loop faster is at a decided advantage; this is referred to as "getting inside your adversary's OODA cycle."

Now compare the OODA Loop to the color code:

White	Yellow	Orange	Red	Black
Oblivious to surroundings	Relaxed awareness	Aware of something (potentially) wrong	Identification of what's wrong and reacting to it appropriately	Combat

Color Codes

Observe	Orient	Decide	Act

OODA Loop

You can see that the two concepts are related. Condition Yellow corresponds loosely to Observe, Orange to Orient, Red to Decide, and Black to Act. These models don't correspond in a direct, one-to-one relationship, but the progression of mindsets and actions they represent are very similar. Because both models have stood the test of time, it's not surprising that they are so similar. Thus, the lesson is doubly clear: you cannot expect to observe a threat or opportunity if you are in Condition White—you must be at least in Condition Yellow. If you fail to observe a threat, then your adversary may have already won the fight because you won't get a chance to do anything else. Therefore, being in Condition Yellow—being able to observe a threat—is a prerequisite for having a chance in any encounter.

IMPLICATIONS FOR TRAINING

Here are three facts about interpersonal conflict for most nonmilitary encounters:

- The average distance is less than five feet.
- The success of tactics is measured in fractions of a second.
- Being aware of the threat is of critical importance to responding in time.

There are two key implications of point #1: First, as we've said so many times, you'll probably have to rely on empty-hand techniques in any sort of encounter unless your weapon is already in hand. Therefore, your empty-hand skills are primary over your weapons skills. Second, should you obtain your pistol, accuracy should not be a problem. However, in real encounters it often is, even at these trivial distances. Why? Simply because people don't practice under stress at these realistic distances in realistic scenarios.

The implication of point #2 is that speed counts! Not just speed, but effective techniques done at speed. A soft punch or a missed shot will have little impact. The lesson here is *drill, drill, drill*. Make powerful technique execution reflexive. This is not all that hard to do—it simply requires "right effort." Too often people work on their 25-yard accuracy with pistols when that precious (and, for most people, rare) practice time could be more practically spent on developing a powerful avoidance maneuver, a fast draw stroke, and accurate point shooting at two yards.

The implication of point #3 is perhaps the most important. You can neither fight nor avoid what you don't see coming. Developing awareness—living aware—is the skill with the most potential payoff. This is not sexy stuff. It requires no gear. There are no competitive or fraternal organizations devoted to it. No one sees you do it or compliments you for having accomplished it. There are no schools to go to and no T-shirts to buy. It's all about you and your own self-discipline.

That's why so few people really work on it.

Think long and hard: If you knew that you would face a deadly-force assault sometime in your life, and if I could wave a magic wand and grant you *either* lifelong, permanent situational awareness *or* Master Class IPSC shooting skill, which would you choose?

TIME, MONEY, AND ENERGY

Ultimately, all we have is time.

Financial professionals remind us that time is money; self-help experts point out that our relative expenditures of time reflect the things we actually value (as opposed to the things we say we value); effort can usually be traded off for time; and some Eastern philosophers even refer to Satan as Time.

So, ultimately, all we have is time—and its derivatives, money and energy. And few of us have it to spare.

Because self-defense is the overarching topic of this book, what happens when you apply the test of time expenditure to your self-defense practice? That is, if you examine the amount of time that you spend on various kinds of self-defense training, what do you see? Do your time, money, and energy expenditures mirror the relative necessities of employing these various self-defense skills? For example, I can concoct peacetime civilian self-defense scenarios in which I would be best served by knowing how to operate a grenade launcher. There is a mathematical probability that I will need that skill; there is not, however, a plausible likelihood of my needing it, so I spend no time on it. In contrast, the most likely self-defense scenarios involve responses with empty hands. (This is even more true when you realize that most lethal-force encounters force you to initially deal with that attack empty-handed.) Yet most people spend little to no time on empty-hand skills, either!

Why? Well, 'cause we like shooting guns, that's why! (At least I certainly do.) And there's nothing wrong with that—nothing whatsoever.

But if self-defense, rather than sport or competition, is your goal, then straight facts and simple logic dictate that most of your time, money, and energy be spent on those skills that you are most likely to need—at least until you have acquired them. As "gun people," we need to avoid the trap of thinking that a gun is the right tool for most of the self-defense situations we will find ourselves in during our lifetimes. (To take this a step further, in order to save a loved one, each of us is *far* more likely to have to perform first aid or CPR than to have to shoot a perpetrator . . . yet how many of us know first aid and CPR?)

Now, that being said (and hopefully the logic being clear), there are some caveats. Yes, acquiring empty-hand skills is the first logical base to cover. However, while these skills take considerable time and energy to master, they don't have to take a lot of money. The nature of empty-hand training dictates that there is not a lot of equipment involved (for the student). Referring to the graph on the following page, gun skills are in many ways the converse. Suitable self-defense guns can be modestly expensive (or not), and sufficient practice ammunition is not free. Quality, responsible instruction in the self-defense use of firearms is not cheap, either, but it is completely necessary. On the other hand, the time required to become competent and safe at realistic self-defense ranges with a handgun, although significant, is usually considerably less than that required to be similarly competent with empty hands. So although you have to invest more time learning empty-hand skills, you may be able to spend less money learning them than

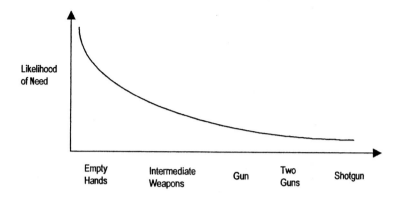

Likelihood of Need

Empty Hands — Intermediate Weapons — Gun — Two Guns — Shotgun

you will during the somewhat shorter time you spend learning handgun skills.

Of course, any one of these self-defense skills can become a hobby, or even a passion. Some of us have devoted a considerable part of our lives to the pursuit of more and more sophisticated empty-hand skills—far more than necessary for most realistic situations. And we all know how addictive the shooting sports can become—again, to a point where the skills acquired are far beyond those necessary to resolve a likely self-defense situation. (Any amount of skill *might* be necessary in any particular encounter, of course—but we're talking about what's likely and the diminishing expected returns thereafter.)

Now, I don't care one way or the other how you spend your time, money, and energy. But I am confounded by folks who spend most of their reserves of these precious quantities strictly on gun skills in the belief that they are better preparing themselves for self-defense. They are doing that to be sure, but in a somewhat skewed way; they are making themselves mightily prepared for one kind of scenario while ignoring more likely ones. If they really were in it for the safety and well-being of themselves and their loved ones, then they would also be acquiring (or have acquired) skill in empty hands, first aid, and CPR.

Carrying and practicing with two guns might be a sound strategy for you, but most people will better spend their time, money, and energy . . .

getting competent at empty-hand skills.

The good news is that street-realistic empty-hand skills are getting easier to find. Twenty-five years ago, one had to search them out and cobble them together from the art-oriented skills that were then prevalent. These days, there is probably a decent street-oriented school in your town. If you live in New York City, check out David James' Vee-Arnis Jitsu School of Self-Defense—one of the best around. Also check out Jim Grover's Combatives Series from Paladin Press; these are some of the best tapes out there on the subject.

Finally, realize that I'm talking about acquiring these skills. Although all self-defense skills are perishable, it requires a lot more effort to initially acquire them than it does to maintain them. For example, you might initially expend a lot of time and sweat acquiring practical empty-hand skills, but then wind down the practice of them to a much less intensive mainte-nance level while moving on to acquiring firearms skills, or vice versa.

The important thing is to be realistic above all else. If you practice self-defense shooting, then you have to ask yourself if you are into it primarily for the *shooting* part or for the *self-defense* part. If the latter, then you should be realistic about what else that entails because time spent on one thing is forever unavailable to spend on another.

Ultimately, all you have is time.

Chapter 8

THE UNFORGIVING MOMENT

As you're opening your car door, your knife in your coat pocket, the nearby young man who was leaning on his car puts you in a choke hold and demands your money—or worse.

You're walking out of the ATM booth, alert for predators. You feel secure with your knife clipped into your front pocket. Suddenly, two of your city's misguided youth dart from around the corner and demand the cash.

It's showtime! Where's your knife? Clipped to your pocket or waistband? Inside your pocket? In your purse or fanny pack? Under your coat? All good places to merely carry it; all bad places for it to be when the curtain goes up.

Few of us live in Hollywood. Attacks aren't duels that are staged at high noon. Today's two-legged predators never learned the rule that says they have to give you fair warning. Assaults happen *fast! Now! Instantly!* And no one can draw a weapon—be it a knife, gun, or baton—instantly. Adding up the time required for threat assessment, reaction time, and actual draw time, you're up to two seconds from concealed carry if you're very good, and often the attack is a fait accompli by then. So what do you do?

Well, you can mostly compensate for these physical limitations with good tactics and proper mind-set. In these examples, alertness and preparedness were the missing mind-sets, and having immediate access to a weapon was the missing tactic.

ALERTNESS

Alertness is the first principle in Jeff Cooper's *Principles of Personal Defense* (available from Paladin Press), a must-read for every student of any defensive discipline. In fact, it's so fundamental that many of us reread it every six months or so.

In the first example, our victim undoubtedly noticed the nearby person and possibly even recognized him as a predator. Yet he or she failed to go into Condition Orange—that state of arousal where one begins to move forward with a deliberate plan of action.

In the second situation,

The pocket-clipped folding knife makes it easy to acquire your weapon—saving much time should it be needed—without presenting it.

the missing attitude (or mind-set) was that of preparedness. You can't be alert to what you can't see (or otherwise sense), as was the case with the wayward youths who appeared from around a corner. However, you can and must be aware of the dangerous possibilities inherent in a situation.

Everyone knows that ATMs are staked out by thieves, and there are almost always lots of hiding places available around them. What the victim should have done as soon as he felt that the stranger was out of place (or even sooner) was have his closed hand on his knife (whether in his pocket or not). Had he done so, his mind-set of preparedness and his tactic of having his weapon in hand would have made his situation survivable.

If you didn't grow up on the tough streets, view Mark MacYoung's tape *Safe in the Street* (from Paladin Press). It's an excellent primer on alertness and preparedness in the context of street smarts.

Weapon in Hand

This is hardly novel or original advice. For centuries, the teachers of defensive disciplines have taught this lesson: *When trouble is or may be near, your hand goes to your weapon.* Today, for example, most cops have their hand on their (holstered) gun anytime they even think that trouble might be close at hand. (This happens far more often than you'll ever notice.) Thus, weapon deployment time is significantly reduced. The same goes for your defensive knife.

Those pocket clips make it easier for you to get your knife into your hand when danger is likely—not when it's coming down. That's usually too late. As explained previously, drawing and deploying even so convenient a knife as a one-handed-opening, clip-carried folder takes more time than a sudden attack usually allows.

In fact, folding knives have a real advantage over guns or even fixed-blade knives in this respect. You can't just unholster your Glock or Cold Steel Trailmaster and stroll to your car through the mall parking lot with it in hand. (You're going to meet some nice uniformed people who will address you as "sir" if you do.) But you can walk to your car, or even down Main Street, with a medium-size closed folder in hand, and no one will even notice.

So what's to lose? When danger is likely—at an ATM, as you walk through a parking lot, certainly as you're unlocking your car door—take your defensive knife out of its hiding place and put it someplace where it can do you some good: *in your hand.*

It's showtime! Do you know where your knife is?

Chapter 9

WHAT ARE WE
TRAINING FOR?

I've just finished Marcus Wynne's page-turner, *No Other Option*. The plot of this book revolves around the fact that one of America's most secret SpecWar operators has "gone off the reservation" and another of his team must bring him down. This is not a typical men's adventure fiction book (of which I'm not much of a fan). In this book the plot is captivating, the mind-set of operators of various sorts is delved into, and the tension between military and law enforcement operators is explored.

Of course, the hero and the bad guy, both top-echelon SpecWar operators, have exceptional physical and weapons skills. Even though Marcus keeps these skills realistic, anyone who tries to keep up on his own physical and weapons skills cannot help but feel inferior to these fictional characters. Contemplating my own age-related deteriorating physical skills and average weapons skills in this light caused me to have one of those blinding flashes of the obvious: that our skills training

John Farnam points out that, for people who don't go to stupid places, don't hang with stupid people, and don't do stupid things, incidents like this random street mugging are their most likely source of encountering violence.

ought to reflect the threats we are likely to face. Ah duh! But wait—it gets complicated for two reasons. One, the word "likely" in "likely to face" brings up a whole world of probabilities, and two, proper skills development for any likely threat is probably more multidimensional than we realize.

What threat are you likely to face? If you are a super-ninja secret-squirrel operator like the hero in *No Other Option*, you may face an entire squad from an elite enemy unit trying to hunt you down. If you are a peaceful accountant living a simple, law-abiding life in Mayberry RFD and have no skeletons in the closet, then the remote possibility of a random mugging or home burglary may be your most likely violent threat. If you are a medical salesperson who carries controlled substances and needles with you, then you may face a premeditated assault by a number of armed bad guys. The police officer, the abused wife, the inner city resident, and you—each face some distinct range of threats along a bell curve of possibilities. For the accountant above to train as a SpecWar operator does would likely be the result of a bad case of testosterone poisoning or Walter Mittyism. For the police officer to train only as the accountant needs to would be a case of wishful thinking.

Plainclothes police officers have their own most-likely scenarios, and they should train differently than the average person.

The first complication in training for your likely range of threats is therefore to understand what "likely" means in your case. Each of us needs to understand the threats that we *could* face, realistically assess what the *likelihood* of each of these individual threats is, and then train for the most likely of them. Going too far afield from the likely threats—i.e., going out several sigma in statistical jargon—is a waste of time from a practical perspective. Your training time is limited; thus, time spent on skills you are not likely to need means skills you could use will not be developed.

Now the second complication in training for your likely threats is that, for most people, many different disciplines will be necessary. To reiterate a point I've harped on many times before, for most up-close, personal assaults, a gun will be of marginal value. Empty-hand and intermediate weapons (OC spray, stick) skills will be the order of the day—either because you have no time to access your gun, because lethal force isn't yet justified, or because you just plain don't have a gun with you at the time. For most people most of the time, it's these *other* skills that will be required when facing their most likely threats. Yet how many gun owners really work on these? How many gun owners foolishly think that having a gun is all they need to be protected?

If I am never going to do a dynamic entry on a crack house, then the time spent training in dynamic entry procedures is very unlikely to be of use to me—and it's taken time away from the empty-hand training that I am far more likely to need. If I am extremely unlikely to face an armed attack by many people intent on killing me, then honing my multiple-target splits represents time that could be better spent on getting trained with OC.

Understand your threats. Assess the likelihood of each of them happening. Be realistic. Be practical. Train accordingly.

Chapter 10

PRIMARY AND
SECONDARY TECHNIQUES

In the last 20 years in the martial arts/defensive tactics community, and during the last 10 years in the firearms community, there has been a great deal of interest in getting "back to the basics." For decades prior we flitted about with fancy art-based systems and complicated so-called scientific or modern approaches to the deadly serious business of self-defense. We spent years in the dojo learning difficult-to-master, counterintuitive movements, and we spent countless hours on the range learning, again, difficult-to-master, counterintuitive techniques. The proponents of these decidedly unbasic techniques argue—with some validity—that they can be extremely effective and that they offer us a greater range of responses than the old-fashioned stuff. They often accuse those who eschew them of ignorance, incompetence, hopeless conventionalism, or laziness.

But the evidence is now in, and it supports a self-defense approach that emphasizes the old-fashioned basics. Today we

57

have decades of evidence that points to the wisdom of this approach, both in the statistics of police use-of-force reports and debriefings and in the study of ordinary street fights. Countless incidents of both types have even been captured on video camera. We also have the experience of genuine force-on-force training (with FIST suits or safe firearms projectiles—neither of which were available long ago). Further, we now have a good understanding of the biochemistry and physiology of stress, and therefore a sound appreciation of what we can expect from our bodies and our minds in a self-defense situation.

Is there room for both approaches—the basics *and* the fancier stuff? Sure. But it's important to understand when each is appropriate (or even possible) and to orient your training around the appropriate response to a given situation. Basic stuff—in both firearms and empty-hand skills—is what is needed for dealing with really dangerous situations or spontaneous attacks. Fancier techniques are appropriate for situations that are not immediately dangerous or where you have control over the action.

The following three examples illustrate this point.

In photo 1A we see a "fancy" response to an attempted punch. This arm-bar throw requires a great deal of skill to execute, and even then you have to get the timing just right. It's risky to try and difficult to implement. A better approach is shown in photo 1B. Here the punch is simply blocked or jammed with an instinctive movement, and the assailant is rushed with a simple strike to the chin—another instinctive movement. This approach has everything going for it under stress: simplicity, aggressiveness, and directness. It feeds off your adrenaline dump and doesn't require fine motor skills or delicate coordination. It is definitely the high-probability way to go.

Now, certainly the arm-bar throw and its ilk have their place in the scheme of things. If the assailant is merely being belligerent or threatening and isn't trying to maim you, then a controlled technique like this might well be appropriate—if you can pull it off. Likewise, if you are initiating action on a

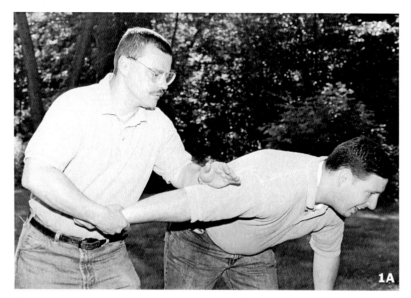

The classic arm bar can be pulled off, but for most people it's a low-probability response.

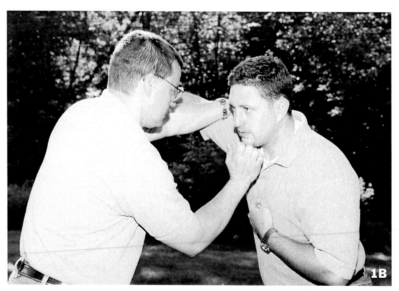

By contrast, a simple simultaneous block and chin jab is easy to pull off and is a high-probability response.

rowdy subject, this sort of control hold might be appropriate to attempt. I even have to confess that I know of at least one black belt for whom this exact technique was his instinctive response to a knife attack—and it worked just like in the movies! That was a lucky day for him. But for most people, most of the time, the next anecdote I think makes the final point: I was in an aiki ju-jitsu seminar that concentrated on control holds and throws like this one. The instructor was one of the highest-ranking masters in this country, and his dangerous day job was bringing in parole violators in a big city. Basically, he was getting into fights every day of the week! I expressed surprise that these "fancy" techniques worked for him in real encounters, and his response was, "They work great . . . after you hit 'em."

Photo 2B shows a primary self-defense technique with a walking cane: Just wap the guy in the groin. Simple, direct, instinctive, and effective—everything you could want. You have to practice to make it powerful, but it's a straightforward technique that holds up well under stress and in the chaos of an assault. Photo 2A, in contrast, shows a technique that's taught in many cane systems as primary, but one that I relegate to secondary status. For this leg sweep to work, your assailant first has to stand still long enough for you to hook his leg, and then the crook of the cane has to be oriented in just the right direction. Of course, you have to hold the cane from the ground end too, and it takes time to acquire this grip. In reality, this is what the wrestlers call a "finishing" technique—something you can do once you are in control of your opponent to finish the fight. But once you are in position to execute a finishing technique, you've pretty much won the fight anyway. Your life and/or well-being are going to be saved by primary techniques like the groin smash.

In photo 3A we see a tactical reload—a technique that is very much a secondary technique in my mind. This is a technique that was originally developed to save ammunition *when you had time to spare or there was a "lull" in the fight.* It was never intended to be a primary method of reloading. Indeed, to my mind, if your gun needs reloading, then getting it stuffed with

This leg sweep is a mainstay of many cane systems, but it is really very hard to pull off in reality.

Here's something much more likely and effective: a groin thrust.

The tactical reload is a technique that the author can see no sense in. Why practice it when most of us get so little practice in . . .

target-focused close-quarters shooting.

Tactical Defensive Training for Real-Life Encounters

potential life-saving bullets is *the most important thing* in the world at that point. So just speed-reload it! If there really is time to spare, you can pick up the partially spent magazine from the ground *after your gun is ready to fight again.* Essentially, I see no need whatsoever for the popular "tactical" reload—I see nothing tactical about it at all. Yet mandated reloads in competitive events are replete with it, and people spend an awful lot of time practicing it.

By contrast, photo 3B shows a much-neglected primary technique: target-focused one-hand shooting. Most fights happen at less than 10 feet, and this is the technique you will need there—and probably the only one you'll be able to coax out of your adrenaline-charged body. Yet very few people practice it, and almost no competitive events specify it. Still, if you're going to have only one arrow in your firearms quiver, this should be it!

There are a lot of self-defense techniques and skills that you can spend your time developing. But before you get too enamored of any one, ask yourself first, "Is this a primary technique, survival-wise, or a secondary one?" If you're in this game for survival, then make sure you spend most of your time on the primary skills. Leave the secondary ones until the primary ones are mastered, or until you simply need some variety in your training.

Chapter 11

IF WE AREN'T SEEING IT ON IN-CRUSIER VIDEOS, THEN WHY ARE WE TRAINING IT?

One of my favorite subjects, the one I harp on most, and one of the few I feel I'm qualified to write about, is the lack of realism in training. In my earlier book, *Defensive Shooting for Real-Life Encounters: A Critical Look at Current Training Methods* (Chapter 1, p. 1), I speculate about the causes of this state of affairs:

> Any physical discipline, it seems, goes through a series of predictable stages. In the early years, practitioners "just do it." There is not a great deal of introspection about how it's done, nor about its various components. One learns by trial and error, or by going to a skilled practitioner and mimicking him or her. Eventually the people with the greatest reputation build up a coterie of followers, and a "school of thought" is born. As with religions, the followers of the great practitioners eventually codify "the (one) way it's done."

Techniques are defined; deviation is discouraged. Other schools are disparaged. Details of technique are isolated and analyzed.

In all of this "progress" some insight is gained, and some advancements are made in the effectiveness of the discipline's practice. But also, context is lost, and the hyper refinement of detail leads to endless internecine struggles and emphasis on the irrelevant. The end goal of the discipline is lost, and its practice becomes the performance of only "correct" technique.

We've seen this progression in fields as diverse as the social sciences (to take a non-physical-skills example) and the martial arts (to use a closer-to-home physical-skills example.) In the social sciences, the original goal of understanding how society is put together and operates has degenerated to the academic mental masturbation that is all too familiar to anyone who has spent time in a university environment. The research is so narrow, its assumptions so artificially constrained, its data gathering so flawed, that the results are doomed to either utter irrelevance or complete uselessness or both. In the martial arts, the goal of winning a violent encounter has been reduced to the practice of artificial kata, gymnastic stunts, and the absence of full-contact sparring from most schools.

The defensive firearms discipline seems to have followed this same progression, too. In the "old days," gunslingers simply did what worked for them, relying on instinct and whatever wisdom they could glean from the men who proceeded them. After World War II, however, the trend toward isolation, analysis, and codification began in earnest in this most personal and most vital of areas. Much that was good came of this, and a good many lives were undoubtedly saved by the insights of those involved. Progress was made, but true progress was soon arrested as the scene became politicized and the inevitable stultification set in.

"Gurus" laid down their gospels, and the discipline made most of its progress in the only semirelated area of sporting competition.

We are much better off today than we were in 1950, but we've plateaued. It's time to move on.

So today we are seeing a "return to the basics" movement in the defensive disciplines. In the empty-hand area, we are witnessing the blossoming of street-realistic schools and curricula. Many of these are based on the insight and experience of men who have been in the cauldron—Fairbairn, Biddle, Applegate, et al. Other approaches, like Jeet Kune Do, strive for the same effectiveness through a more sophisticated and more time-consuming path. When I started out in the martial arts in the early '70s, I had to spend a lot of time searching out the rare teachers of street-effective techniques and cobble them together into a street-realistic system as best I could. There were but a few thousand like-minded souls, at best, around in this country at that time. Now I can find a school in almost any town that teaches in a couple years what I struggled for decades to pull together. Progress—not in the "art," but in realism and effectiveness—has definitely been made by returning to simplicity and focusing on the brutal, messy facts of a violent encounter.

Likewise in the firearms disciplines. We have seen a great resurgence of interest in so-called point shooting—again, a technique developed by men like Fairbairn and Applegate. Although the debate rages on about the merits of point vs. sighted shooting, the fact remains that in some cases—up-close, spontaneous encounters—we will simply not be able to focus on our sights at all. *(I need to point out that while this last statement is true, most writers invariably follow it with the statement that this is because we are unable to focus our eyes at close distances under extreme stress—which is false. When bad guys stick guns into the faces of victims, the victims have no trouble later describing the exact details of the gun [and the bullets in it, if it's a revolver]. What is true, however, is that we are hardwired to focus on our threat during extreme stress.)* If we are unable to see our sights during close, spontaneous attacks—and more than half the deadly attacks on law enforcement officers occur within five feet—then to teach a sighted response to this situation is criminal. When we start from the reality and facts of the situation and then work backward to training methods—instead of "starting from a conclusion"—we are faced with the necessity of incorporating point shooting at close distances into our firearms training.

Let me close with a brilliant and insightful quote. I recently spent a day at a course by Tony Blauer at the Smith & Wesson Academy. Tony is a hot commodity these days; he teaches his brand of street-realistic empty-hand defense to marquis law enforcement and military agencies worldwide, and he's booked years in advance. Tony said, "If we aren't seeing what we're teaching our officers on the dashboard-mounted video camera recordings of violent encounters, then why are we still teaching it?"

Chapter 12

CARNIE TRICKS

"Carnie"—the word refers to itinerant carnival workers who make a living by cheating the carnival goers. They use sleight of hand and rigged games to separate their marks from their money. It all looks so legitimate that you can't figure out what happened . . . but you often feel that something "just ain't right."

The same types of carnie tricks have been long used in the martial arts, too. In these, the game is to pass on dubious "self-defense" techniques to well-meaning but innocent students and get paid well for it. Everyone wants to be able to defend themselves, so there are marks a plenty to go around. And with what you pay for a one-, two-, three-, or five-day seminar . . . or months or even years on end of instruction, there's plenty of money to be made.

Dubious, unlikely, and downright phony techniques abound in this game, but they tend to fall into four major categories. Here's a look.

THE BIG BLACK BELT RINGER

In this con, the instructor demonstrates a "self-defense" technique on the biggest black belt in the room . . . and pulls it off elegantly. Slam! Bam! Woosh! The big guy falls. "Wow," everyone thinks, "if this technique works on that big, skilled dude, it has to work on lesser assailants." The technique in question can be anything; the con comes from the fact that the instructor has rigged the game by selecting a "ringer" from the audience—someone who will allow him to pull the technique off. How is this possible, given that the instructor and the big black belt may never have met?

Well, the size of the black belt is irrelevant. It's just cosmetic, and the big guy was chosen for his fearsome appearance. The heart of the con here is to choose a black belt from the audience to demonstrate on—the higher the ranking, the better the con actually works, and the more effective the alleged technique appears to be. Why? Because you don't get to be a high-ranking black belt in any traditional martial art without having two things burned into your subconscious.

First, you are instinctively a good *uke*—you just can't help but cooperate with your partner to make a technique come off smoothly. The necessity of "helping" your partner to make a technique work has been drilled into you for years, and you've practiced it tens of thousands of times. Second, respect and deference to authority—at least in the dojo—has become a way of life for you. You'd no more think to foul a guest instructor's demonstration of technique than you would to spit on the training mat. You automatically go along with what the technique is supposed to do.

Put these two factors together and you can see that, from the perspective of the carnie instructor, the best way to show a technique working—and simultaneously the best way to impress students with its "effectiveness"—is to demonstrate it on the biggest black belt in the room. It'll work like a charm every time.

One of my "favorite" techniques in this category is the knife disarm. You know, the one where you block the incoming knife attack, trap the wrist or arm, and knock the knife out of your assailant's hand. If you don't realize it already, this is all but impossible on anyone who isn't cooperating. Yet the world of martial arts is full of similar techniques that students pay good money to learn. Unfortunately, too many of them find out the hard way, on the street, that they were dupes.

The way to see if a technique *really* works? Those of us males in this business with wives who couldn't care less know one critical test: try it out on her! No one makes me look worse, or fouls more of the things that I try, than my untrained wife!

THE NO-FIST-SUIT SWITCHEROO

Only because I've not heard this before, I call it Mroz' Law: *Anything at all will work at 1/2 speed and 1/2 force, most things will work at 3/4 speed and 3/4 force, a surprising number of things will work at 7/8 speed and 7/8 force, but almost nothing works at full speed and full force.* That is, any set of motions at all—taken from ballet even—can be made to work as a self-defense technique at half speed and half force. There are certainly enough impractical martial arts (e.g., the drunken tsetse fly style) out there to attest to this. (There's nothing wrong with studying an art—just don't confuse it with practical self-defense.) Most of those "techniques" can be made to work at increasing speeds and power, too. The reason for this is that the person making the technique work still has the extra time and energy between whatever speed and force level his/her partner is working at and full speed/full force as a buffer. That is, if my partner is assaulting me at 7/8 speed and 7/8 force, all I have to do is to slip into 15/16 speed and force for a moment to "beat" him and make the technique appear to "work."

But almost all techniques fail at full speed and full force. This is for two reasons. First, things certainly get harder as you increase speed and force, and this is as high as you can turn the dial. Second, there is no way for the instructor to apply more speed or more force than the other person is applying, and thus cheat his or her way to making the technique work.

I don't want to pick on any particular style here in giving an example, and honesty forces me to admit that I have (well-trained) friends who can make some very unlikely techniques work better than I can make simple, proven, direct ones work (for example, I have a friend who can repeatedly kick my head almost faster than I can punch). But the rule of thumb is that if the technique isn't simple, brutal, unsophisticated, and direct, it probably has a low probability of success when the rubber meets the road.

The mantra for realistic training is *full speed/full force*. Which means we need a way to practice full-speed/full-force technique safely with our partners. The FIST suit is still the only protective equipment on the market that allows safe full-speed/full-force training and provides acceptable mobility. If your instructor doesn't use FIST suits in training, then there's no way to know if the technique will work for real—that is, at full speed and full force. Most instructors don't. Don't you wonder why?

THE FLASH FINISH MISDIRECTION

This con reminds me of the old Steve Martin joke: *How to make a million dollars and pay no taxes! How, you ask? Well, [said very fast] first-make-a-million-dollars, and [now speaking normally] then when the time for taxes comes, just say you forgot!* I hope the punch line here comes through in print: the hard part of the job (making a million dollars) is glossed over, and then your attention is directed somewhere else.

There's a lot of "self-defense" technique out there that's like this, too. It consists of masking the very unlikely nature of a technique by directing your attention to a series of flashy and powerful finishing techniques. The concept of practicing more than a couple techniques in succession has always amused me anyway—as if there's some way to predict or direct a fight in a choreographed manner, or as if you'd want to deliver a dozen crippling blows after the first. But this teaching method can be used profitably by the self-defense carnies. First-you-intercept-his-fist-in-mid-blow-by-applying-the-secret-elbow-lock, and then you knee him in the groin, elbow him in the neck, drop an axe kick on the spine, and break his arm as you throw him to the ground. Oh—and you can stomp his shin once he's on the ground, too.

One good example of this con is a complex joint lock used as a primary technique, followed by any number of follow-up breaks and locks. Let me comment on that in this way: I have had a well-known, very high-ranking jujitsu practitioner, whose particular law enforcement job required him to be in almost daily fights with arrestees, tell me that joint locks work great . . . so long as you hit the perp hard first!

Basically, a technique has a high probability of succeeding or it doesn't. If it doesn't, all the follow-up techniques on a hapless and submissive partner (on which these are invariably demonstrated) can't change the fact. Don't be fooled.

THE PHONY DISTANCE BAIT-AND-SWITCH

This con is the easiest to detect because it can't be disguised. Nonetheless, countless people fall for it every day because they are baited by the promise of an effective technique and switched to an impotent substitute for it. The con here is to perform a technique at an improper distance. Usually, the technique in question is demonstrated six to nine inches too far away. Take a look the next time you see a demonstration or read an article. You'll see "counters" to punches that are landing in the empty space inches in front of the defender. This particular con is endemic in knife-on-knife or counterknife technique demonstrations, which are almost always shown with the attacker's knife coming nowhere near striking the defender. Perpetrators of this con will say that they are simply demonstrating the technique so that it can be seen clearly (as if you or I couldn't see it if it were six inches closer).

What's happening is really much more underhanded. Things become very difficult when the attack is realistic. They are much, much easier to deal with when the attacks are landing not on the defender but in the empty space in front of him. So many more things can be made to "work" when one has the luxury of not actually getting hit, and when one has extra space in which to work.

You should call your instructors on this. Ask them to perform their technique at *realistic* fight distances. Often they won't want to because 1) fewer things actually work there, 2) what does work there seldom looks elegant, and 3) even things that can work there fail more often. Fights are messy, and even the winners don't look pretty or cool. That's too much realism for too many instructors. It's much easier to dance in the empty space.

There aren't too many "bunko" squads anymore, but the old-time cops will tell you that you have to know the con to beat it. Likewise, if you are to avoid falling victim to the martial arts carnie tricks, you have to know them, too. Here we've covered the four most common types. Take the material you've been studying and examine it for traces of them. Play with the specific techniques that you suspect of being cons, and come to your own conclusions.

It's your life.

Section 3

EDGED
WEAPONS

This section is devoted to knife issues. The knife is a great self-defense tool, and one that we can have with us almost all of the time. It is instinctively deadly, yet its effective use in combat requires training. This is not a book on knife skills—as in using a knife for self-defense—and these are not addressed here. There are many excellent books and tapes available on the subject, and the main source of them is Paladin Press. Rather, the chapters in this section address some of the peripheral issues of knife-based self-defense.

Chapter 13

KNIFE BASICS

I have occasionally been involved in a task in which it was inconvenient to access my own knife and have asked someone next to me to borrow his, only to get the response that he didn't have one. Every time this happens, I am simply shocked, having carried at least a small knife with me every day since I was four or five years old—in the city and in the woods, in a business suit and in uniform.

It's bad enough when regular people don't carry so much as pocketknives anymore, but it's unthinkable that a police officer wouldn't.

Carry a knife! Why? Well, for the same reason that you carry a pen in your pocket and flares in your cruiser. You never know when you'll need it, whether for some chore or for a lifesaving emergency. You just know that you will sometimes need it. Knives are used for everything—from opening donut boxes to gathering evidence to freeing victims caught up in ropes. I'm told that knives have even been used to cut seat belts in order to free trapped victims, although I doubt that this actually happens much. And whereas undercover cops have been known to rely on a knife for self-defense when they couldn't carry a gun, I have heard at least one (secondhand) story about a patrol cop who wouldn't have been injured if she'd had a knife accessible as a last-ditch weapon. But for the most part, knives are utility tools for police officers. And unlike their SWAT counterparts, who need a strong fixed-blade knife that can function as a pry bar (think of prying open windows or floorboards), most police officers are well served by one of the incredible variety of well-made 2 1/2-inch to 5-inch folding knives on the market today.

THE GOLDEN AGE

This is, in fact, probably the golden age for knives of all sorts, especially folders. There were a few custom knife makers in the United States prior to 1970 (with Bo Randall of Randall Knives probably being the best known), but for the most part the knife market then was a pretty staid and stable one, occupied by a few well-established manufacturers, each with a defined niche. Then, starting with a mere handful or two of top-quality custom makers in the early '70s, the custom knife movement began to grow exponentially. Today there are literally hundreds of them, and there are thousands of second-tier makers. And all this was happening at the same time that the martial arts and self-defense boom was hitting. What this combined explosion did for the average Joe or Jane was to plant the seed for three trends that are in full bloom today: 1) it jump-started the creativity of the industry, causing the established manufacturers to update their designs and make them more suitable for other-than-hunting markets; 2) it spawned a new breed of manufacturers devoted to high-quality knives, mostly for "tactical" (self-defense, survival, emergency services, military, etc.) purposes; and 3) it engendered the collaboration of top custom designers with volume manufacturers, so that a maker's heretofore

The classic Randall knife that started a revolution. This is still one of the author's most valued and practical knives.

expensive, custom-made designs could be made available to the general public at affordable prices. And we haven't even touched on the advances in materials (including steel) that occurred during this period.

The bottom line is that today there are more superb knives available at competitive prices for any imaginable application than at any time in history.

WHAT KIND OF KNIFE DO YOU NEED?

The bad news—if there is any—is that choosing a knife is now seemingly more difficult than ever. There are just so many of them with so many different features. Should you buy a knife with a spear point or tanto point blade, made from a 440 steel or ATS-55, with a lock-back or liner-locking mechanism, with a "tactical" or utility design? And what's the real difference between a $40 knife and one costing $200 anyway?

Stay tuned. All (or almost all) will be revealed—at least to a practical extent. But first, let's put this all in perspective. Man has existed for a million years with the knife as his primary tool. *Any* knife that you can buy at your local hardware store today is so far superior to the tools that man relied on for—literally—survival for more than a million years that our long-ago ancestors would have considered it worth killing for. And just about any decent knife that you buy today is of a quality that your grandfather could—again literally—only fantasize about as a young man. All of the knives from quality manufacturers are excellent by any rational—and certainly any historical—standard. Be glad you have this difficult choice.

So, what's the ideal knife for a police officer? Well, it depends. (Sorry, but that's the truth.) It depends on your job, your environment, and you. We've mentioned SWAT team members as probably better served by fixed-blade knives. A similar argument could be made for game wardens, officers who spend a lot of time in the wilderness (some aspects of the Border Patrol come to mind), and those in other specialized law enforcement jobs. But the vast majority of police officers—uniformed or not—will find that a general-purpose "tactical" or utility folder will be ideal. A word on the word "tactical"—this is a marketing invention. It has been applied so liberally to anything that someone wanted to sell that it has now reached the point where it means everything . . . and therefore means nothing. So I won't use it anymore here—I'll use more specific terms instead.

Blade Shape

There is a difference between the ideal blade shape for general utility work, self-defense, precision cutting, hunting, and any other task. In police work, a knife will see use as a utility tool mostly and as a self-defense tool very rarely, if at all. The spear and drop-point shapes (and dozens of variations on them) are probably the best all-around utility choice. The tanto shape is very popular and is arguably stronger than any other, but it is really less useful for general

The tanto profile (top) is less practical for general utility work, in the author's opinion, than the usual drop-point blade below.

utility work in my opinion (although it has its share of proponents who disagree with me).

Steel

Every steel used in production knives from the top manufacturers is great for all-around use. Stain-resistant steels (so-called stainless steels) have chromium in them to resist rusting, but chromium is very hard, and these steels are generally more difficult to sharpen than nonstainless, sometimes referred to as "carbon" steels. (*All* steel is made from iron, carbon, and other elements—with the specific additional ingredients and the recipes for making them being different.) Nonetheless, most good folders these days are made from top-quality, stain-resistant steel. Some of the more common industry-standard steels you'll see on these knives include 440A, 440C, AUS6, AUS8, AUS10, BG-42, ATS-34 (aka 154-CM), ATS-55, and many others. In addition, many manufacturers apply their own marketing name to the steel they use, so you don't really know what the steel is. Two of the more common industry standard non-stain-resistant steels in use are D2 and 1095, and, again, there are lots more.

It's important to understand that all of these steels will give excellent performance. Non-stain-resistant steels can be kept rust-free with just a moment of maintenance—especially with Sentry Solutions products (discussed below). But if you work around water—particularly salt water—a lot, then stain-resistant blades are definitely the easier way to go.

Steel is a coarse granular structure—and the degree of the granularity will determine just how close to a theoretical straight line a sharp edge ground from that steel can get—that is, how jagged the edge will be when viewed under a microscope. Therefore, different steels feel and cut differently even when sharpened to as sharp as they can get at the same angle. And of course, knives can be sharpened at various angles, either in a straight line ("straight grind") or along a concave line ("hollow grind"). The edge grind is referred to as the "edge geometry," and it makes a difference in performance. Also, the blade itself can be ground in various cross-sectional shapes, and this also affects the way the knife cuts different materials. The bottom line with regard to blade and edge geometry and the particular steel used is that for extreme tasks they make a difference worth worrying about. However, for everyday use in general utility work, all of the common good steels work.

The main difference that you'll see in knives as you use them on the job is how often you have to sharpen them, and that depends on how hard they are. Steel hardness is measured on the Rockwell scale, and most good knives have "R" values in the high 50s to maybe 62. Harder isn't always better. Harder means longer edge retention, yes, but it also means more difficult to sharpen. And harder can mean more brittle in some cases. (The opposite of brittle, in steel lingo, is "tough"; toughness refers to the ability to withstand shock and impact.) You will have to sharpen your knife sometimes anyway, and it's not difficult. The good news is that the harder steels tend to be more expensive, so an easier-to-sharpen knife will often be easier on your pocketbook with no effect on field performance. If you want to get all nerdy about the steel in your knife, great—have at it. But my advice is there are more important things to worry about.

Finally, realize that knives are ground from steel as it comes from the foundry and then heat-treated. This heat treating is as important—maybe more so—than the steel used in determining the knife's properties. All of the top manufacturers have excellent heat-treating capabilities these days.

Locking Mechanism

In the good old days (the early '90s), there were only two locking mechanisms in common use: the lock-back and liner lock. While in theory the liner lock can be made stronger, in practice it depends on the design of the knife (how thick the liner is, how deep the blade detent on a lock-back is, etc.). And it depends on how well the knife was manufactured. Back then it wasn't uncommon to have liner-locking knives come out of the factory with poor tolerances, which meant that the knife didn't lock up well. Today, manufacturing quality in all respects is much better than it was 10 years ago, and the last few years have seen a plethora of new, innovative locking mechanisms, most of which make a claim to extra strength. The bottom line here, though, is that all of these mechanisms are strong only with respect to a force applied to the spine of the blade, and they are all strong enough. Equally important as far as actual folding knife use goes is its lateral strength (how well the knife resists breaking when force is applied perpendicular to the flat plane of the handle), and all folding knives are weak here. This is the Achilles' heel of a folder. So the thing to actually worry about in choosing a folding knife is how easily the locking mechanism can release when a tight working grip is applied to the opened knife—which depends as much on your hand size and fleshiness as it does on the knife's design. Try this on any knife before you buy—you'll be surprised at how easily some knives can accidentally close on your fingers! The best knives,

The liner-locking knife at the top has a much-exposed liner release, which can accidentally release when you least want it to! The Bob Kasper design below does not have this problem.

in my opinion, have their unlocking mechanisms recessed so that accidental releases can't happen. Such knives are uncommon, though.

Handle Material

All materials in common use are fine. G10 (fiberglass), Micarta, Kraton (rubber), Zytel (glass-filled nylon), and a host of others all work fine for utility knives. Inherently smooth materials such as G10 and Micarta should have a coarse surface to provide a good grip. Tacky materials such as Kraton are even better for grip purchase, but they can hang up in a pocket or sheath.

Serrations

Most utility knives these days come in a choice of a straight edge or a half-serrated edge. Although I (slightly) prefer a straight edge for defensive knives, when you need serrations, you do, and they're great to have for some everyday tasks.

Coatings and Finishes

Knives come in two basic finishes: polished and bead blasted. The polished finish is more rust-resistant because it has fewer cavities for water to collect in. Knives are also available in quite a variety of coatings—mostly black, and all serving to retard corrosion. Now there really *is* quite a bit of difference between the lower-quality coatings and the high-quality ones, but that difference isn't very important in terms of the use that a knife will get in the hands of the average police officer. And because the price of the coatings isn't always proportional to their performance, I wouldn't worry about it. Just treat your knife with Sentry Solutions' Tuf-Cloth.

Construction

I've mentioned a lot of things that really don't make much of a functional difference to a working cop, but the knife's construction does because it determines the knife's working life—that is, how well it will hold up. The cheapest ($10) imported knives that you sometimes see are really nothing more than badly ground, non-heat-treated cheap steel, with the blade and handles held together with a couple soft pins. These knives are certainly dangerous and can kill you in the hands of an assailant, but they will last only for a few jobs if you use them yourself, and they'll do those jobs badly.

Knife construction varies in many aspects, including whether pins or screws are used to hold the knife together, if washers or ball bearings or something else lubricates the blade pivoting surfaces, how thick the pivot pin is and of what material it is constructed, what kind of bushing surrounds the pivot pin, how well-mated the bushing and blade materials are, and so on. What you pay for in a knife—in addition to the blade and handle/scale materials—is the quality and cost of the construction. You get what you pay for, but for most POs, a simple but quality construction will usually perform well.

Bottom Line

What all of the above adds up to is that a basic knife from one of the top manufacturers will probably be perfectly adequate for most cops. But make no mistake: there's joy of use and pride of ownership in well-made tools. Therefore, more-than-basic knives of high quality are what many of us have opted for.

MAINTAINING YOUR KNIFE

Sharpening

The best knife in the world will need sharpening, so you might as well get used to it . . . and in fact, it's quite easy. There are a lot of good sharpening products on the market made from all sorts of materials—India Stone (aluminum oxide), silicon carbide, waterstones, diamond, and ceramic—and they all work well if the right tool is chosen for the job. But I'll make it easy for you. For bench sharpening, the experts almost all use a combination of medium-grit Crystolon (silicon oxide) stone and fine grit India Stone from the Norton Company. In an 11 1/2-inch length, this combination stone is Norton product number IC11, and its inexpensive price is far less than many fancy contraptions that you can buy. The Norton Company's marketing of its sharpening stone line is somewhat sporadic, so you may have to look around a bit to find one—woodworking suppliers are a good bet. The rule of thumb is to use a stone as long as the blade you're sharpening, and for a couple more dollars, live it up and get the longest one available. Note that this particular stone (the IC11) is prefilled, meaning that it has been soaked in liquid paraffin to fill its pores. Thus, the oil you use in the sharpening process (WD-40 is a good bet) stays on the surface of the stone where it does some good, rather than soaking into the stone. Not all of Norton's stones are pre-filled, and most competitive stones aren't either—but it's a *very* valuable feature. Sharpening stones are low-tech and cheap—buy the best.

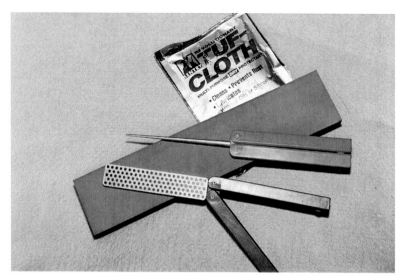

Everything you need to maintain your knife: a Norton India stone, Diamond Machining Technology DuoFold diamond hones, and a Sentry Solutions Tuf-Cloth.

For sharpening in the field, light weight is critical. Diamond Machining Technology's Diafold sharpeners are the ticket here. Get a double-sided Diafold in extra-coarse/coarse grit (model number FWCX-017042011635) and a fine grit Serrated Sharpener/Conical File in a Diafold configuration (model number FSKF-017042 011055). These items are light and inexpensive, require no lubrication (or you can use water), and are very effective.

Lubrication and Rust Resistance

The way that you maintain your tools says a lot about you, and your knife is no exception. Fortunately, knife maintenance is extraordinarily simple. When it gets dirty, rinse it off and dry it. Use a small drop of good oil at the pivot pin every now and then. And wipe the blade every so often with Sentry Solutions' Tuf-Cloth. Tuf-Cloth is a long-lasting, lint-free replacement for oil and silicone rags. Instead of using oil, Sentry uses a mixture of dry film corrosion inhibitors and lubricants to provide a fast-drying, water-displacing, microbonding crystal barrier. This stuff really works, and despite the fact that a Tuf-Cloth costs only a few dollars, it's used worldwide by special operations forces who can carry anything they want, and it's endorsed by more than 40 knife and tool companies. Sentry has recently introduced a complete knife-care kit containing a Tuf-Cloth, a tube of Tuf-Glide (its high-tech, fast-drying lubricant/rust-inhibitor), and a small GATCO ceramic sharpener—all in a handy pouch.

Chapter 14

KNIFE OR GUN?
SOMETIMES THERE'S NO CHOICE!

Why would anyone carry a knife—one of man's oldest weapons—for personal defense, instead of man's 20th-century personal defensive weapon, the modern handgun?

Well, there are lots of reasons. Here are five of them:

1) *Maybe you can't get a permit to carry a gun.* That's good if you're a con or a dangerous person. For the rest of us (the potential victims), that's bad. Some states simply have no provision for civilians to lawfully carry a concealed handgun. In states that do, the process required to actually exercise that right can often be a challenging to impossible one.

2) *A knife is easier to carry.* No question here: knives are lighter and smaller than guns. A lightweight folder weighs only a couple of ounces and is considerably smaller in all dimensions than the smallest reasonable-caliber handgun. Even a large Bowie knife, such as the

Cold Steel Trailmaster, weighs less than the lightest two-inch snub-nose revolver when loaded (17 ounces for the Trailmaster vs. 16 ounces for an unloaded Smith & Wesson aluminum-framed Model 442). You don't have to make any special provisions to carry a knife—such as wearing a coat, heavy belt, or holster. You just slip it into a pocket or the waistband of whatever you're wearing.

3) *A knife is as fast as a gun.* Drawing a one-handed-opening folder or a fixed-blade knife can be done just as—or nearly as—fast as drawing a gun from a holster, and much faster than drawing a gun from deeper concealment, such as an ankle- or belly-band.

4) *A knife can travel with you.* Even if you have a permit to carry a handgun in your home state, you probably don't in other states you visit. This goes double for trips outside the United States. If you want a legal weapon, a good knife is practically your only option. When you are traveling by air, you can carry practically any size knife to your destination legally in your checked baggage.

5) *A knife is legal to carry in most places.* The state and even local laws regarding which knives are legal to carry and which are illegal vary considerably. I used to think that a four-inch blade was a safe bet anywhere, but I have since found that 3 1/2-, 3-, and even 2 1/2-inch limits on concealed folders are common across the country. Also, many jurisdictions differentiate between mere possession of a knife (in your house, for example) and public carry, between fixed-blade and folding knives, between single- and double-edged knives, and between spring-opening knives (switchblades) and regular folding knives. For example, here in Massachusetts, switchblades and double-edged knives (defined as a knife with any part of the back sharpened) are illegal to merely possess, whereas there is no legal restriction on the length of blade that you may carry in public, either

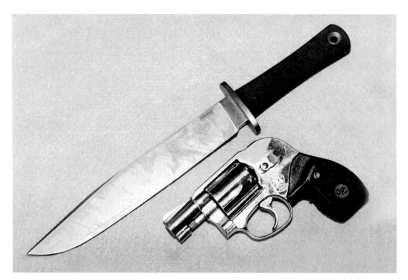

The large Bowie knife (a Cold Steel Trailmaster) weighs less than a fully loaded lightweight snub-nose revolver.

in plain sight or concealed. The only way to find out for sure what laws apply in your state and city is to go to the law library at your local courthouse and research the issue. My experience at several of these is that the staff librarians are very glad to assist "regular" (non-lawyer) citizens. Just make sure you ask for assistance when they aren't busy helping the lawyers and court personnel who regularly use the library.

So knives are not poor cousins to handguns. They have distinct legal and tactical advantages, and, unlike guns, you can almost always have one with you.

Chapter 15

KNIFE DEFENSE–
TWO APPROACHES

Edged-weapons attacks on police officers are both common and easily accomplished. After all, knives and other edged weapons are available for a few dollars anywhere, so we have to assume that every person we encounter is carrying one (most of *us* are!). It follows, then, that one of the basic skills an officer should have is unarmed defense against a knife.

Why *unarmed* defense? Hasn't it been drilled into us that a knife is a deadly weapon and that it should be met with our deadly-force option—our firearm? Well, yes . . . if you have time. That is, if someone threatens you with a knife, or you are responding to an incident in which you know that a knife is being used in an assaultive manner, then you should definitely have your firearm drawn and challenge the potential assailant with it.

But life isn't like the movies, or even, often, our training scenarios. Real-life knife attacks are typically sudden and spontaneous. Since it goes without saying that a spontaneous knife attack will happen at very short distances, it naturally follows that you simply won't have time to draw your firearm in this circumstance. (Life isn't fair!) *You will therefore have to defeat this deadly-force attack with your bare hands.*

You probably were taught some sort of response to this situation at the academy, and if you were lucky, it may have even made sense. But unfortunately, too many of the empty-hand skills taught to police officers are simply wishful thinking. Things are definitely getting better in this regard, but there are still too many armchair defensive tactics being taught!

Here's the test: unless you got to practice your knife-defense skills at *full speed and full force* against a FIST suit-clad,[1] knife-wielding opponent, you'll never know if they'll work until the real thing happens. That's a bad time to find out.

UNDERSTAND THE DEPTH OF THE PROBLEM

But before we talk about empty-hand counterknife techniques, let's set the context.

First, empty-hand defense against a knife attack is *the most difficult problem* in defense tactics and the martial arts. Steven Segal's theatrics notwithstanding, this is a very hard thing to do!

Second, the brutal truth is that a committed spontaneous knife attack by a trained knife fighter at close distance is all but impossible to defend against. That scenario is not a fight; it's an assassination. The lesson here is to keep your guard up, watch suspects' hands, pay attention to the clues that are almost always present, and keep distance (or some object) between yourself and someone you don't know. Third, expect to be hurt . . . and to fight through it and win! One of the cardinal rules in a knife fight has always been that you should expect to get cut, and it's true. Some instructors lately are saying that we shouldn't prepare our students for failure by telling them this. My opinion is that we should prepare our students for reality, and teach them to deal with it! After all, if you were in a fistfight, you'd expect to get hit—and no one will tell you differently. So, if you find yourself defending against a blade, expect to get cut and to have to visit the hospital afterward. But also expect that you will win that fight and live to go to the hospital!

Fourth, forget about all those joint locks that you've seen people (sadly, including some law enforcement instructors) teach. *They do not work for real people in the real world!*[2] If you doubt this, get out your training knife and try them at *full speed and full force* (nothing else really counts, does it?). I'm not usually virulent in my writing, but this is too important to be polite about: *any instructor that still teaches joint locks in response to a knife attack is a dishonest fraud who's putting his ego above your life!*

TWO APPROACHES

There are basically two practical approaches to the empty-hand knife defense problem that work. As with any physical skill, they can't be instructed through an article—but we can outline the gist of the two approaches and point you to sources of instructional information.

The first approach is outlined in a video, *Facing the Blade* (no longer available), which Jeff Kunz and I made in the early '90s. We made that video because even though we had studied the knife arts for years, we were dissatisfied with all of the knife defenses we had been taught. Since that tape was made, our approach—called the Avoid, Control, Destroy, Cover, or ACDC—has been picked up by several touring law enforcement instructors, to our gratification. The ACDC approach consists of initially avoiding the incoming knife, controlling the knife arm, applying massively destructive injuries to your assailant in order to shut down his ability to fight (this is a deadly-force encounter), and then seeking safety for yourself and any bystanders afterward. In the tape,

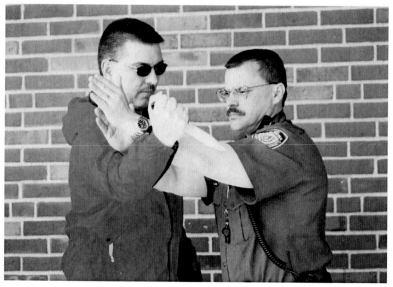

The first step in the ACDC counter-knife system is to avoid the knife—here with a block.

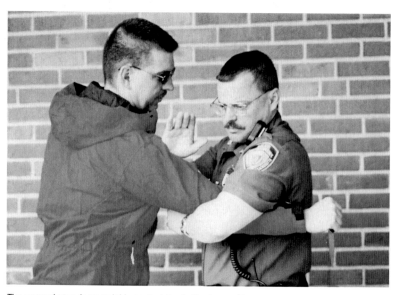

The second step is to quickly control the knife—here with an arm wrap.

Tactical Defensive Training for Real-Life Encounters

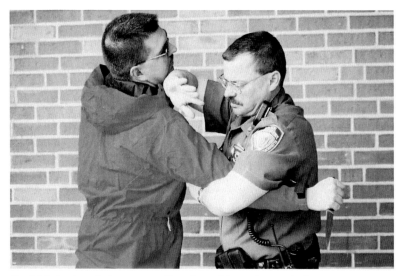
The third step is to destroy your assailant—here with an elbow to the face.

we walk the viewer through the angles from which a knife attack can come, and through avoidance techniques for each of those angles. We then introduce the two controlling techniques that we have found to work long enough to give you time to counterattack: the *grab* and the *wrap*. And then we show you many of the destructive techniques that can be applied to shut down your attacker from various grab and wrap positions. Real-life situations are simulated, along with full-force/full-speed application of the ACDC system. We often don't look pretty in these simulations . . . but that's the way life is!

The other approach is the more traditional one of avoidance and immediate or simultaneous counterattack, without the controlling element employed. The best advocate of this approach is David James of the Vee Arnis Jitsu School of Self-Defense in New York City. Professor James inherited the Vee Arnis Jitsu system from the famous Professor Vee, and his

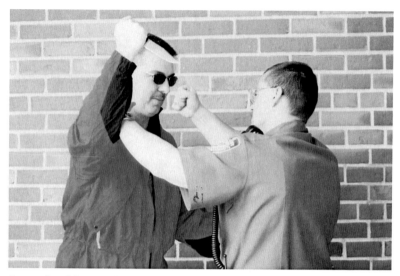
An equally valid approach is to simultaneously avoid being cut (here with a block) and stun the attacker.

school is the best self-defense-oriented school in New York. The approach he uses is similar to ours in terms of understanding angles in order to avoid the initial knife attack, but he then advocates an immediate and intense counterattack. In fact, David disagrees with our approach of attempting to control the knife arm at all. Although we suspect that not controlling the knife arm makes it likely that the attacker can cut you before you can shut him down, David—after demonstrating an avoid/counterattack combination on his tape—turns to the camera and says, "The address of this school is 25 Park Place, between Broadway and Church. If you think you can cut me after I've just hit you like this, then please come down here and show me."

David James is a friend and a much, much better martial artist than I am. If I lived in New York, his school is where I'd be studying, and I give full credence to his opinions. His dedication to his students, his commitment to the protection of the innocent, and his enthusiasm for his subject matter jump right off the screen in his tapes, which are available only to law enforcement personnel through FIST Inc. (www.fist-inc.com).

A WORD ON EQUIPMENT

Like any defensive tactics skill, knife defense needs to be practiced with intensity and, eventually, at full force and full speed. You will need two pieces of equipment to do this.

The first is a FIST suit. FIST makes a line of protective suits that protect the wearer from full-force blows with hands, feet, or baton. Your simulated assailant needs to be wearing one so that you can go "full out" in your defensive practice. If you've never done this, you'll be amazed at just how difficult it is compared to even 3/4 intensity defenses. At a few hundred dollars, and lasting almost indefinitely, a FIST suit is both a necessary and an affordable investment for anyone serious about survival.

The second thing you'll need is a good training knife. The ideal training knife is neither too rigid (impact and thrusting injuries can easily occur at even less than full force), nor too soft (a trainer that "flops," or collapses too easily on impact, is not realistic). Thus, while metal replicas of your actual knife and drones (actual but dulled knives) are practical for empty-air practice, force-on-force training requires a knife that's "rigid enough" but not so rigid that it will injure your partner. The best trainer I've seen is made by Bill Lewitt. It's made of 1/2-inch neoprene die-cut to the shape of your knife. Inexpensive and invaluable.

THE ACID TEST

Remember that the defensive tactics field is full of armchair theorists and that almost anything will work at 1/2 speed and 1/2 force, many things work at 7/8 speed and 7/8 force, but few things work at full speed and full force.

Remember that the acid test of any technique is in the three Fs: FIST suit, full speed, and full force.
Practice with honesty and stay safe!

END NOTES

1. The FIST suit is still the only equipment on the market that allows nearly full mobility to its wearer while withstanding full-force blows.
2. OK, I actually know a few people who can make them work. But these are extraordinary people with 30 years of full-time training in the martial arts. They are not you; they are not me.

Chapter 16

FALLACIES OF KNIFE SELF-DEFENSE

There are all kinds of (sometimes contradictory) myths, half-truths, and fallacies surrounding the use of a knife for self-defense. Although many of these fallacies understandably exist as oft-repeated "common knowledge," others, not so understandably, are perpetuated by unknowledgeable self-defense "instructors." Sometimes these instructors or writers are simply full of hot air, sometimes they are just plain ignorant, and mostly they haven't studied knife fighting. Let's set a few of these fallacies straight.

FALLACY #1: I need a supersharp, extrastrong knife.
FACT: The criteria for a good defensive knife are different from the usual "hack down a sapling and still shave hair" routine that applies to camp knives. A knife used in self-defense needs to be sharp, but it only needs to cut your assailant a couple times to do the job—after which it will be confiscated by the police. A purely defensive knife needs to be strong enough

Two excellent defensive knives at different ends of the size spectrum: a Spyderco Endura and a Becker Knife & Tool Combat Utility 7.

to not break upon hard contact with bone, but it does not need to be able to pierce steel or hack through car doors. But make no mistake about my meaning: high-quality, supersharp knives from quality manufacturers will definitely make your defensive job easier.

FALLACY #2: Any old knife will do for self-defense.

FACT: Any old knife is probably capable of killing someone, if that's what you mean. But a defensive knife has to be brought into action quickly—hence the need for a one-handed-opening folder or a fixed-blade knife carried in a speed scabbard. A knife used in combat should have a guard to prevent your hand from slipping down on the blade when it encounters bone. A defensive knife should ideally have nonslip handles because blood is very slippery. And finally, a knife used for fighting should be balanced appropriately to your fighting style. A style favoring flicks, for

Proper training with a knife will increase your chances of using it effectively in an emergency. Arnis practice is a mainstay of both stick and knife skills.

example, is better served by a knife balanced at or just behind the index finger, while a style favoring heavy hacks or slashes will be better served with a knife with a balance point farther forward.

FALLACY #3: A knife is so simple to use that you don't need training with it.

FACT: Anyone can use a knife with deadly effectiveness if he or she takes a victim completely by surprise. But to use a knife to extract yourself or your loved ones from danger in a defensive scenario (that is, from a situation you did not initiate) is a different matter. Your opponents may have weapons themselves, there may be multiple assailants, and almost certainly you will be facing people who are extremely dangerous. In these cases you must have trained in similar circumstances yourself to know what to do, and you must have practiced repeatedly to ingrain that response.

FALLACY #4: You don't need to learn empty-hand techniques if you carry a knife.

FACT: You may not always be able to get to your knife; not all situations will allow it. Even if you can, you will probably need to create the time and distance necessary to draw your weapon; remember that you can easily be surprised by an up-close attack. In any case, the situation may de-escalate during the confrontation, and although the use of your knife may no longer be justified, less lethal force may still be called for.

FALLACY #5: You always go for the body's vital points in a deadly-force self-defense encounter.

FACT: The extremities will usually be easier and faster to reach, particularly if your assailant is grabbing for you or holding onto you. Deeply cutting your assailant's arms, hands, or legs will partially shut him down, or at least go a long way toward discouraging him. Also, your assailant's hands may be wielding a weapon, and the wisdom of thousands of years of life-or-death edged-weapons struggles indicates that you first want to make those weapons dysfunctional by disabling the hand that controls them. "Defang the snake," as the Filipinos say.

FALLACY #6: I need to carry a really big knife for self-defense.

FACT: Big is good but small is fine. Proficiency with a weapon is far more important than the particular weapon utilized. A small, three-inch knife can slash and penetrate sufficiently to disable an attacker, particularly if you are trained in knife defense (see point #3 above). In any case, realism dictates that you will probably be carrying a three- to four-inch folder.

FALLACY # 7: I need a double-edged knife for self-defense.

FACT: A double-edged knife or dagger is a fine instrument for self-defense, and it does possess some advantages over a single-edged knife. However, a single-edged blade will do just fine in a defensive scenario, and its disadvantages vis-à-vis a double-edged dagger all but disappear in trained hands. Remember that you don't want to be tied to any particular knife or knife design for self-defense; you want to be able to pick up any available edged weapon and use it instantly and effectively.

FALLACY #8: I will get the Good Citizen of The Year Award if I kill an assailant with my knife.
FACT: You will probably be arrested and put on trial. Expect it and accept it. If you were justified in using lethal force, you will probably be exonerated, but only after a lengthy ordeal. Learn what to do and what not to do in a lethal-force confrontation—this is not something you can learn on the job. You can begin by reading *In the Gravest Extreme* by Massad Ayoob; although it focuses on the use of firearms, its discussion of lethal force is relevant to any situation

Chapter 17

THE IRRATIONAL RATIONALE OF THE TACTICAL KNIFE

Today we have "tactical" everything—guns, knives, boots, gear, suspenders (I'm not making this up), and so on. I suppose someone even markets "tactical underwear" (interesting possibilities there). I even write for a magazine titled *Tactical Knives*, which is a very good magazine indeed. Yet, according to Webster's, tactical refers to "the specific means of accomplishing a goal." By that definition, my coffee in the morning is "tactical"—it is a specific means that I employ to wake up; my slippers are "tactical"—they are the specific means by which I avoid popsicle toes.

All I can say is that the guy who started all this "tactical" nonsense—sometime in the '80s, I think—should be writing Madison Avenue copy or inventing pet rocks. The adjective sure has caught on, eh? The problem is that now that it means everything, it means nothing.

Actually, I'm being a bit of a curmudgeon. Just as with another linguistic abomination, the ubiquitous "hopefully," we all know what is meant when the word tactical is used: mean, action, SWAT, SEALs. You know.

I guess we're stuck with it.

So, herewith, a little expose . . . ahem . . . exposition on the "tactical knife."

THE STEEL DOESN'T MATTER

These days, we have a bounty of high-tech steels available to knife makers and manufacturers, all damn near approaching the holy grail of long-lasting edge retention and easy sharpening. Actually, there will always be a trade-off between these characteristics and those of toughness and stain resistance. AUS8, a steel that your grandfather would have given up your father's children for, is no longer good enough for today's sophisticated knife crowd. Even ATS-34, the mainstay of the high-end market for a decade, is now almost passé. Today, we have to have BG-42, ATS-55, or one of the other new wunder-steels. These are very good steels, certainly. Sexy, yes. Expensive, too. Makes you the envy of your neighbors.

But do you need them?

To answer that question, you have to consider the mission of your "tactical knife." The always-present-even-if-unsaid assumption when talking about tactical knives is that they can or will be used as weapons. This is certainly a legitimate use of the things. But consider the quality of the steel in that context. How many people are you gonna cut with your knife, anyway? I mean, you'll use it *once*, and it will be seized as evidence.

So here's the deal: For a knife carried (virtually) exclusively as a self-defense tool, the steel doesn't matter. So long as it has an edge, you aren't going to reuse it enough to make edge retention an issue. In practice, maybe . . . but there, frequent sharpening is not a real concern. (And if you practice at all, you're in the minority of folks that carry knives for this purpose.)

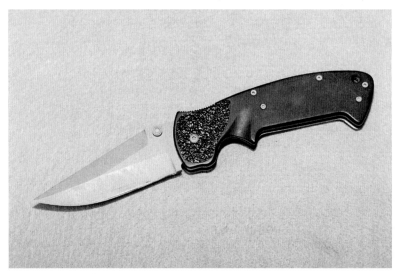

The Kasper Folding Fighter is the pinnacle of defensive folders.

THE STEEL MATTERS

Yes, it does. There are some knives, like Bob Kasper's designs, which are intended to be carried and used solely as self-defense weapons. Although Bob's designs, in their current executions (as of this writing, by makers Al Polkowski and Pat Crawford and Columbia River Knife & Tool), are made of top-tier steels, they would fulfill their intended purpose equally well if made from kitchen knife steel.

However, there is a whole other area of "tactical knives" for which the steel can be critical. I'm talking about military knives, backwoods knives, survival knives, and so on—knives that are seldom used (if at all) as weapons but see extensive use as tools, cutting and otherwise. For these applications, resharpening can be an unwelcome field task. Imagine a deep-sea diver having to stop and resharpen his knife, and you get the idea. Here, the demands of the environment and application will dictate the optimum knife shape, edge geometry, and steel. Here, the choice of steel can make the difference between, at one extreme, convenience and inconvenience, and at the other extreme, survival and missing tea time.

Also, many, if not most, of the "tactical knives" on the market are designed to be used as both a utility knife and possibly a self-defense weapon. Here again, the criticality of steel choice is proportional to your degree of utility work with said knife.

BLADE SHAPE IS IRRELEVANT

In the realm of self-defense, this is, for all practical purposes, true. A knife requires almost no skill, power, or coordination to be used with damaging effect. Hurting someone with a knife is simplicity itself, and *once the knife is in your hand*, any knife will do. (Where skill, power, and coordination *are* important in a self-defense scenario is in getting yourself into an advantageous position to employ the knife, or in extracting yourself from a disadvantageous position. Of course, the greater your skill with a knife, the more sure you can be of your success once you use it. And if it's a knife-to-knife situation—which is very rare—then naturally skill with the blade is critical.)

The emphasis in self-defense should be in getting the knife into your hands (and opened if it's a folder). We're talking contact distance here, and as with another lethal-force option at contact distance, the gun, speed of weapon acquisition is a bit more important than skill at weapon deployment. With contact-distance shooting I don't dwell on marksmanship. I worry about maneuvering into a position to actually draw the gun, and I worry about the speed and sureness of that draw. Likewise with the defensive knife.

The most critical aspect of the defensive knife is *the speed and sureness with which it can be acquired under stress.*

Most instructors dwell on the easy (albeit necessary) skills of using the knife *after* it's in hand. This is, to put a fine point on it, cheating the student. The hard part, the part that everyone glosses over, is *getting the knife into action.*

Using your knife to defend against a blunt instrument is more likely than against another knife. So practice, practice, practice.

Which brings us back to Bob Kasper (and no, he's not paying me). Now, I have used the word "best" only twice in my knife writings over the years—once in a utility knife context, referring to the KP-TOMMI line of pukko knives from Kellam Knives, and once in a defensive knife context, referring to Bob's designs. Bob's knives are unique in that their acquisition has been completely thought out. What this means in practice is that the handle of both his fixed-blade and his folding creations are designed from scratch to get the knife into your hand fast—and to keep it where it belongs once it's there, when you need it most. I don't know of any other knives made that do this so effectively.

THE KNIFE IS THE EQUAL OF THE GUN

Obviously we're talking self-defense situations here . . . and actually this is true, so long as we are referring to each weapon's effective range. That's about a step or two steps' distance for the knife and, well . . . out to wherever, depending on your skill and the particular firearm under discussion. It's worth keeping in mind something Mas Ayoob has often said: "Within a second, a pistol can put a few half-inch holes in you. A knife, by contrast, in that same time, can completely vivisect you." This is why, if forced to make the awful choice (and it is a lousy choice), many of us would prefer to be shot than stabbed.

So clearly, a "tactical knife" is an excellent choice for a self-defense weapon if you can reasonably expect the assault to be up close, which is where most self-defense situations occur and where most defensive gunshots are fired (54 percent within five feet). However, the knife is *merely* the weapon. Yes, *merely*!

As a lot of self-defense teachers have taught, survival in a hostile environment is due to four factors. In order, from the most important to the least, they are 1) awareness, 2) tactics, 3) skill with your weapon, and 4) the weapon itself. Just as with a gun, it's *far* more important to have an adequate weapon and practice a lot with it than it is to have a better weapon with which you practice less, if at all. With the gun, most experts advise buying a good one and spending your extra money on practice ammunition. With a defensive knife, buy a good one and spend the extra money on lessons in its use.

Also like a gun, a knife is all too easy to carry as a talisman—like a good luck charm. I'm not talking about the obvious stupidity of carrying it in a purse or glove box (although too many people do just this). I'm talking about assuming that your knife and the moves you learned with it are sufficient to arm you. The operative word in "knife fight" is *fight*. The knife is only your hardware. It's controlled by your software—in this case, your knowledge and skill and, more importantly, your fighting spirit. A good instructor can show you how to use a knife in a relatively short amount of time. Inculcating a true fighting spirit, however, is much more difficult and takes a lot longer (if it's possible at all) if you don't come prepackaged with it. Attitude beats skill (usually).

As is the case with any other weapon, acquiring a defensive knife is merely the first step in arming yourself. You need the right attitude. You need awareness skills. You need to learn the right tactics. You need to learn the knife skills themselves. And although the knife is a significant advantage in a confrontation and can be an equalizer, you must *still* know good, solid, practical unarmed skills. The knife supplements these—it does not obviate their necessity.

You will probably be surprised in an assault (or should at least train for that distinct possibility), and thus there will simply not be time to get to your knife to deal with the attack initially. You'll have to deal with that initial assault with your empty hands, and then create the time and distance to draw and deploy your knife. And that may not even be possible. The ugly truth is that many attacks happen so close in and unexpectedly (despite good awareness skills) that your empty hands will be your only available weapons. The knife is not a shortcut. Good self-defensive skills come from mixing it up in the dojo, from getting hit, from sweating.

All of this is equally true for the gun. So, in both its positive aspects *and* in its shortcomings, the knife really is the equal of the gun.

A Tactical Knife is Really Something Quite Plain

This whole "tactical" thing too often takes the form of appealing to young men's testosterone-fed fantasies. Consider the tasks that a "tactical knife" will, in most applications, perform: cutting random materials, defending life and limb, prying things, digging holes, probing, puncturing things. Now, there are two reasons a knife that will do all of these things reasonably well will, in most cases, be a fairly plain one.

First, any unusually shaped knife will be very task-specific. Nature is stingy, however, and there's an inherent trade-off between excellence at a single task and good performance at

These two classics, the KA-BAR and the pukko, are also exemplars of utility.

many. A "tactical knife," by any reasonable or common definition, has to be versatile.

Second, we have to remember that the knife is man's second oldest tool. It's been around for a while. And for most of mankind, the knife that was carried all these years was there to perform tasks that we now differentiate and call "tactical" (which tells us just how far from a natural life we've come these last hundred years). Throughout the centuries—millennia, actually—most of mankind has used some pretty simple blade shapes for the variety of tasks on which life depended. History is there to learn from.

So most of the classic and time-proven "tactical knife" designs are reasonably simple and straightforward. Consider the KA-BAR and the pukko. These two basic designs—a slender Bowie and utter simplicity itself—are the parents of almost any time-proven or practical tactical knife design in use today. Indeed, these two designs continue to be widely used as they are. There are exceptions, of course. (Bob Kasper's designs are purely and solely devoted to the specific task of self-defense—so they aren't exceptions.)

So there's the irrational rationale for the tactical knife. The steel both matters and it does not. The blade shape is irrelevant. The tactical knife is the equal of the gun. And a tactical knife is indistinguishable from an ordinary knife.

Section 4

FIREARMS

T his section is about firearms and firearms
training. It can more or less be considered
to be a set of "extra" chapters to my previous
Paladin Press book, *Defensive Shooting for Real-
Life Encounters*. These chapters are all based on
articles I have written since the publication of
that previous book, and I thought their content
was timeless enough to warrant inclusion here.

Chapter 18

BACK TO THE FUTURE

I write this just hours after returning from a day of Massachusetts State Police (MSP) in-service firearms training. This training, like all of the MSP's new firearms training program, was devised by Mike Conti, the director of the department's new Firearms Training Unit. Mike is one of the new breed of superb trainers who base their training on the reality of gun encounters, and thus reach back to the wisdom of a previous era for some of their material.

Military training of the early 20th century was primitive by today's standards and concentrated mostly on marksmanship against paper targets. Later, Fairbairn and Sykes, who worked in the close-quarter combat cauldron of Shanghai, devised an unquestionably street-relevant and effective form of pistol training for police. The Shanghai police won a lot of gunfights as a result. Applegate achieved similar results with it in World War II. For some reason in the post-World War II era we once again became fascinated with marksmanship and the hitting of static paper targets, albeit with more macho-looking poses and with high-tech, sexy-looking guns. Disciples of the then-new "combat" competitive shooting subsequently entered law enforcement firearms training in droves and with the fervor of St. Paul converted on the road to Damascus. Police training today is still largely influenced by this school of thought, and we are still shooting at static paper targets.

The only problem is that police still aren't hitting the real guys they shoot at.

Can you guess why? It would be obvious to a Martian! It's because real gun encounters don't faintly resemble shooting in formal poses at little pieces of paper! That anyone ever thought such artificial training could actually help us survive real encounters is . . . well, I guess "delusional" would be the most polite, accurate word. Would anyone advocate learning to box by "sparring" with paper targets? The necessity of actually getting in the ring with a live opponent is too obvious to require explanation. Why should it be different with guns?

Mike on the East Coast, like Lou Chiodo on the West Coast, was struck by the fact that something like 80 percent of rounds fired by cops miss, and that 75 percent of them are fired within only 10 feet. Yet traditional police training shoots almost no rounds at less than 10 feet. Something was clearly wrong . . . if not downright stupid.

Mike's training consists of instruction in Applegate-style target-focused shooting at close distances (as well as sighted shooting at longer distances), and he has re-created a version of Applegate's famous "house of horrors." In this "house" the shooter is forced to navigate real-world problems in real-world conditions (such as low light). Three-dimensional moving good guys and bad guys appear suddenly, and shoot/don't shoot decisions must be made instantly under body-alarm reaction. Badges are mistaken for guns here, and startle reaction causes the "good guys" to get shot. Yet if you wait too long to identify your target, you risk getting shot yourself. It's often damned if you do and damned if you don't. Just like real life!

As I write this, about 1,000 people have been through MSP's "House of Horrors," and none were able to use their sights. Most have stated that they didn't use them because they had an overwhelming feeling that "there was not enough time," even though there really was. Memory lapses, tunnel vision, and auditory exclusion are common experiences, and so are mistaken memories of events.

Mike first put MSP Detective Bureau personnel and brass through this course, and the result was a lot of "Wow . . . when I've interviewed witnesses or even investigated officer shootings and come across these lapses or mistakes, I usually assumed the person was lying or being evasive. I wish I knew then what I know now!"

Video simulators are also used in the MSP program (on the same day, even, so you can get a good comparison of the two training methods), and they are just not the same at all. These video simulators are a good way to develop verbalization and judgment skills, but even they don't come close to the real-life simulation of the House of Horrors. They are a step in the right direction, but not sufficient.

Anyone who tells you that you can use your sights in a *spontaneous close-quarter* encounter simply hasn't done the homework of actually going through a realistically simulated one. Likewise, anyone who faults an officer for a mistaken-identity shooting under these dramatic circumstances simply doesn't have the experience to know what he or she is talking about.

How much longer will we continue to fool ourselves? It's time for us to thoroughly reform our firearms training, including going back to the future for some of it.

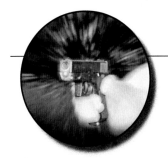

Chapter 19

DEAD PRETTY:
TOXIC DYSFUNCTIONAL TECHNIQUE

Way back in the . . . well, way back when, when I was just coming up in the martial arts, we still practiced such elegant techniques as the crescent kick to kick a knife out of an attacker's hand and the four-corner throw to disable a knife-wielding assailant. These were truly cool-looking pretty-boy techniques, and all the Hollywood martial arts stars used them. Now, of course, street-realistic practitioners don't bother with these kinds of techniques at all because we "know" that they just don't work. (Although honesty compels me to tell you that I have two personal friends who did, in fact, defeat knife attacks with a crescent kick and a four-corner throw, respectively, I also have to point out that they themselves admit that they were young and foolish at the time . . . and damn lucky, too!)

What had happened in the martial arts was that the constantly used war skills of the European and Asian cultures that have influenced us eventually devolved into an art-centric form

A crescent kick against a knife seems silly, and it is.

of practice, as peace became more the norm. As we went from *martial* skills to martial *arts*, the practicality of the content diminished. Then, in the 1960s a young turk named Bruce Lee (following in the tradition of earlier men like Fairbairn and Applegate) made pure street-practical technique his passion, and he started a revolution in the discipline of self-defense. It was back to the future as the tide turned back to truly effective practice. In the '70s and '80s I had to look hard to discover people who could teach me the various elements of purely practical self-defense; now all that knowledge that I worked so hard to find has been thoroughly systematized, widely disseminated, and passed on to a new generation. Today you can find a pure street-realistic school in your area as easily as you can a classical, traditional judo dojo.

We in the gun business can learn a lesson from our martial arts brethren here.

The *martial* skills era of handgunning existed from roughly the mid-19th century to the 1950s. Subsequently, the martial *arts* era of handgunning had its place in the sun until the 1990s. As with the empty-hands arts, self-defense handgunning is now going back to the future with a renewed emphasis on pure street-practical technique. As with the empty-hand arts, we have the advantage this second time around of so much more scientific knowledge about how human beings function, and the intelligence and experience of those so engrossed is now networked via modern media and communications technologies.

And also as in the empty-hand arts, we still have a lot of *art* passing as *martial* skill. We still have a lot of ineffective "pretty" techniques being taught—the crescent kicks and four-corner throws of the handgun world. What follows is a look at five of them. I need to add that like the crescent kick and four-corner throw that worked for real for my friends, the following techniques have also certainly worked for real. That's not the point—anything can work sometimes. The point is that they are *unlikely* to work, and we know better today.

The Erect Weaver Stance

The Weaver stance has been beat to death over the last decade. Although it does have its respectable holdouts (my friend and teacher, the redoubtable John Farnam, for one), almost no one uses it anymore—either for competitive shooting or self-defense work. It's complex, unnatural, and tends to fall apart under body-alarm reaction. The entire argument against it is perhaps best delivered in Andy Stanford's excellent book *Surgical Speed Shooting* (Paladin Press, 2001). Yet it is still taught. I admit that it certainly has its place in the scheme of things—mainly building searches, because the confined space there forces you to flow continuously from one position to another. But as a primary platform for shooting, it's widely discredited. Yet it definitely looks macho, cool, and pretty. Dead pretty.

Stationary Shooting

Most range practice consists of drawing and shooting.

When under attack, you will be moving. That's how you should practice!

Stationary drawing and shooting, that is. Yet if there's anything that in-cruiser videos and years of force-on-force simulation training has taught us, it's that lateral movement is perhaps the most effective tactic we can use at realistic (that is, real close) gunfight distances. Defenders who move laterally tend to get hit a lot less than those who . . . well, just draw and shoot. Shooting while moving looks sloppy, though, while staying stationary makes you look—just like those pictures of competitive shooters you see in the gun magazines—under control and pretty. Dead pretty.

THE
HAND-MEETS-HAND-IN-THE-CENTER-OF-THE-BODY
DRAW STROKE

It's almost gospel at shooting schools that in a proper draw stroke, the support hand "waits" for the gun hand to meet it near the sternum, and the gun is then presented with a two-hand grip in a straight line to the target from there. That is most definitely the best way to get accurate, fast, repeatable shots on target . . . but not necessarily "on assailant." In the close, confined, and chaotic environment of a fight for your life, your "targets" aren't usually several yards away from you, nor are they stationary. They are close in and coming at you! They are probably so close that an extended "presentation" will either result in a contact shot (and possible jam) or your disarmament. Your support hand will probably be quite busy fending off the attack and buying the fraction of a second you need to get your gun into play. Time is well spent practicing this kind of realistic, sloppy, chaotic self-defense. Alternatively, you can practice very photogenic and pretty range skills. Dead pretty.

GOING FOR THE HEAD SHOT

There are still instructors out there advocating head shots as a "failure-to-stop" technique. I know and like some of them, but I disagree with them here. The logic I apply here is simple: Either the guy who's "failed to stop" is *real* close to you and thus you *might* actually be able to hit his moving head while you're hopefully moving also and you're both hopped up on some serious blood chemistry. Might happen. Except that if he's that close and he ain't stopped, then he's going to be on top of you quite soon, so maybe something other than your trusty pistola is called for at this point.

Or he's so far away that *maybe* you have time to hit his noggin before he closes in on you—except that he's still moving, so are you, and the distance is now so great that it's a real problematic shot, especially with what you *have* to assume are innocent people all around. There are certainly exceptions to the two possibilities I've painted here, but they are just that—exceptions. Head shots are for snipers . . . and pretty boys. Dead pretty.

STAGING THE TRIGGER/RESETTING THE TRIGGER

I admit—on this one I don't have enough experience with simulations to say for sure, but then, during force-on-force exercises I'm not under full-blown sympathetic nervous system override anyway, and I know I'm not going to get hurt. But it seems to me that the fine motor ability to both stage and reset the trigger is one that's going down the flusher for sure under body-alarm reaction. I know that these are supposed to be the "secrets" to fast, accurate shots—and for competition or paper target shooting that's all great. Relying on them to hold up in a spontaneous fight for your life, however, is doubtful. Furthermore, staging the trigger seems to violate a primary rule of safety: *Keep your finger outside the trigger guard until you have made the decision to shoot, are on-target, and are actively engaged in shooting.* I simply don't know how the advocates of trigger staging get around this one unless we're talking about slow distance shots—which is not generally the case in self-defense. I'd like to be corrected on this, but for now these techniques seem like more pretty-boy stuff. Dead pretty.

Real fights are dirty, messy, sloppy, and in your face. Technique is secondary to tactics and aggression. No one looks good in them, and everyone often gets hurt. Trying to look pretty is not an appropriate goal.

ONE HANDGUN DRILL:
MAXIMIZING YOUR
SURVIVAL CHANCES IN PRACTICE

Life takes its course. Some years you have lots of time for
an activity, and some years (or decades) there are other demands
on your waking hours. As my time for range practice has diminished these last few years, I find myself compensating (to a
degree) by focusing only on pure survival skills when I get to
the range. During this time I've also been honored to make
friends with many survival experts. Putting two and two together, I sent them the following question by e-mail: "What *one*
handgun drill do you consider to be the most important for
maintaining *survival* skill with that weapon?" Notice that I said
survival skill, not gun handling skill. Their responses follow.

Dave Spaulding's response and reasoning was the same as
mine would have been:

> The one drill that I always do is draw and fire. I do it
> at 20 feet [7 yards], thinking this to be the outside limit

of the majority of handgun encounters. I use an 8-inch plate, thinking that this is the proper size target to approximate the vital area in the high chest region. From the tactical side, it helps me practice getting on target fast from the holster. There is more to the fast and accurate draw than many believe. It requires a consistent arm movement, consistent grip, consistent movement to the target, and consistent trigger press and follow-through. You get a good return using this drill for the time spent. I like to see a concealed draw/hit accomplished in 1.5 seconds, though I don't push speed—I prefer accuracy.

Mas Ayoob:

The way I begin and end every practice session of my own is what I call a "focus drill": at four to seven yards, one magazine into one spot on the target, no time except "reasonably quick," with the purpose being all shots in one hole. This seems to refresh the hardwiring of neurolinguistic programming of what is needed to make a perfect shot, and makes certain that the basics are still there.

Gabe Suarez:

At any distance: Move laterally as you draw (so that the lateral move coincides with the first shot or trigger press), press twice or three times. Stage for and take the head shot if it's necessary. Move laterally again. Assess the target from the contact ready position. Ask yourself, "Did I hit him? Did it work?" Scan along a 360 from the "sul" position and ask yourself, "Does he have any friends?" Return focus to the original target and execute a tactical reload.

Bob Taubert, recently retired from the FBI's firearms training unit:

Since 95 percent of shootings take place within 30 feet, I like the one-handed presentation, married to the multiple-hit point-shooting technique.

Mike Boyle had a similar response to Dave Spaulding's:

1) Use a target with a realistic size "A" zone five to seven yards away. (Closer threats may require an empty-hand response, and while threats at longer ranges are very real, they are less likely.) 2) Draw and fire a pair of shots ASAP. I don't associate any magic quality in the firing of pairs; however, I feel that is all I might be able to get off in real life. More might be better, but one is likely to run out of time before bullets. 3) Run the drill facing target, left face, right face, and about-face. Threats appear from odd angles. 4) Work with gear actually worn. 5) The ability to break the Gunsite par of two shots in 1.5 seconds is great, but it is far better to recognize danger sooner. Don't get too hung up on time, but strive for a fumble-free, accurate response. Speed will come with smoothness. 6) Mix it up. Run it one hand and in poor light. I often use paper plates as targets.

Lou Chiodo, who has saved a lot of lives these last several years, offers this:

At the root of this drill are target-focused shooting skills, since the worst-case scenario is that the attack is spontaneously initiated by the suspect. Engage the target while moving laterally. This gets the shooter out of the suspect's "kill zone." This drill is done at contact distances to approximately seven yards. The starting positions for this drill include a combat ready position, a close-quarters ready position, and a holstered position. The movement is practiced in two ways. Rapid movement is used for situations where the terrain or circumstances allow us the distance and ability to move freely. A slower movement

Moving off the line of the attack is the proven way to up your chances in a typical gun-fight.

technique is also practiced for situations where the environment does not allow rapid movement. *The goal in close quarters is to move off the line created between you and the attacker* [Ralph Mroz' emphasis]. This drill is practiced in all lighting conditions, with and without the use of a flashlight, and with one- and two-handed shooting grips. The accuracy goal is 100 percent hits on the Training Protocol Target (TPT) that I developed and which is available from Qualification Targets (www.targets.net).

Mike Conti, who directs the Massachusetts State Police Firearms Training Unit, has a reality-based program that includes a Col. Rex Applegate-style House of Horrors (which, I can tell you firsthand, is very humbling):

> The one survival pistol drill I wouldn't leave out is the one-hand pistol refunction drill. Our research at

One-hand (including weak hand) firearm refunction skills are critical, since your gun (and gun hands) will attract bullets in a gunfight.

the MSP FTU (House of Horrors program in particular) indicates that hand/arm gunshot injury is frequently caused by the natural body-alarm reaction/adrenaline dump, causing perceptual narrowing—tunnel vision—onto the threat or perceived threat. As the eyes lock onto the threat, the rounds often follow. Therefore you must have the knowledge and ability to clear and reload your pistol while using only one hand—and with either hand for obvious reasons.

Andy Stanford of Options for Personal Security offers this:

I like John Farnam's basic test. Stand seven yards from a silhouette target with your gun loaded with six live rounds and one dummy. The dummy should not be the round in the chamber or the last round in the magazine. Fire six body shots, clearing the dummy with a "tap-rack" when it comes up. Then reload from slide lock and fire two head shots. Move when not firing and during all weapon manipulations. Communicate with the ersatz assailant before the drill ("Stop!"), when drawing ("No!"), and when reloading ("Drop the weapon!" or "Back off!"), and practice talking with witnesses and responding authorities after the drill. Zero misses and at least 50 percent hits in the vital zone is a good minimum standard. An accomplished shooter should be able to keep 90 percent of his hits in the vital zone. Farnam requires 100 percent in an IPSC "A" zone or equivalent, but I feel this excessively slows down everyone except master- level shooters. A rough guide for acceptable times is as follows:

- Start signal to first round: 2.5 seconds beginner, 2.0 intermediate, 1.5 expert, and 1.25 master.
- Split times between body shots: 1.0 beginner, 0.5 intermediate, 0.35 expert, and under 0.25 master. For head shot splits, add 0.25 to listed body splits; for beginners add 0.50.
- Malfunction clearance: subtract 0.5 from above draw times.
- Reload: add .75 second to above draw times; for beginner add 1.25.

Bert DuVernay, former director of the Smith & Wesson Academy, related his favorite on-duty drill:

I have the luxury of a range that approaches 180 degrees of fire, so I set two targets at a wide angle, start verbalizing, move, draw, fire several shots at the first target, move, several at the second, move, several at the first, sometimes moving and firing again at the second. I repeat this until I've exhausted three mags, so I work in some mag changes. Sometimes I'll include the J-frame in my pocket when the slide locks back. Then I reload my duty ammo, get back in the cruiser, and drive off. Life is good in a small rural PD.

Harry Adams, the well-known Boston-area instructor, offers this:

> I draw from a concealed (never exposed—what's the point?) holster, firing three rounds at five yards (that's the distance that the threat will most likely be when I begin shooting, if I'm lucky and alert), hitting the yellow area in a S&W target with all rounds and moving laterally several yards in case the rounds aren't effective and the threat keeps coming. I try to do it fast, naturally, but feel that the entire drill, with solid hits, is more important than an ultrafast time. Besides, if I achieve solid hits, I won't have to shoot again.

Hoch Hochheim has been evangelizing a street-realistic, integrated weapons approach to defense for years. He advocates concentrating on proficiency in a close-quarters retention shooting position:

> Shooting stats show that most pistol fights occur in extremely close quarters. A two-handed grip, traditionally involving punching the handgun forward, allows for a lot of countering opportunity. I believe in the training concept of "fighting first, systems second." I believe that all combat shooters must start in the CQC range first, battling their way through quick draws under the stress of an enemy, nose-to-nose. After this block of training is mastered, then we move out to more traditional modes and distances.

John Peterson, formally of the Sigarms Academy, goes for a more complex drill that must be seen to be understood:

[This drill] integrates threat ID, verbalization, immediate movement, a draw from concealment or duty rig, two-hand shooting, pivot, shooting on the move, shooting from cover, reloading at cover, moving to new cover, and multiple opponents in multiple directions. In some classes students start this drill from a chair, or disabled, or from a vehicle. On a disabled run, they go through the drill single-handed and they still do the emergency refunction. The backup gun can be incorporated as well. It is a good drill also to go into cold, and it can be done in a low-light variation. *I think that anything that combines more than one essential task is a step in the right direction* [Ralph Mroz' emphasis].

Clyde Caceres, director of training for Crimson Trace and a respected trainer, has this to say:

Be able to present your weapon smoothly and quickly and direct it at the threat. Be able to orient your weapon in many ways other than simply the traditional square range methods. Engage does not always mean shoot. Train to evaluate a threat quickly and engage instantly only if necessary. The martial art of shooting has its foundation in assessment, reaction, and movement. Almost everything important, with the exception of accuracy, can be drilled in dry-fire environments. I practice with visual feedback tools like the Crimson Trace lasers to indicate my muzzle control, safety, and accurate presentation with dry-fire, enabling me to synthesize training in unusual (read realistic) ways.

Walt Rauch had a different take on my question altogether, and one that's well worth ingraining:

You alone must clean your personal defense weapon, load the magazine(s), or charge the cylinder and recharge the arm. Never, under any circumstances, allow anyone else to do any or all of these tasks. If the arm leaves your possession for any reason, you must recheck the system before using it. Trust me, I have good reason for this absolute rule.

So there you have it—straight from the computers of 14 of the leading survival experts. Note the emphasis on close distance, fast first shots, and movement. Note also the emphasis on combined skills—you can't just stand still, draw, and shoot a couple rounds. Train as you fight!

Chapter 21

THE MARLIN .357 LEVER-ACTION GUN FOR HOME DEFENSE

I don't know who first coined the term "home defense gun," but it's become part of the standard lexicon in the firearms media. A gun's appropriateness for "home defense" has thus also become a standard consideration for many gun buyers, and many of them have one or more firearms dedicated to this task. But what is "home defense" anyway; how much of it is realistic . . . and how much of it armchair fantasies?

I'm of the "keep it simple" school. Although I do own more than one gun, I also realize that my practice time is too limited at present to become really proficient with more than one of them (and sometimes I fall short of my standards even there, I'm afraid). For that reason, my present "home defense gun" is the same plastic wonder-nine that I carry both on duty and concealed. It's stored in a Mossberg InstantAccess safe under my bed when it's not on my hip. This arrangement assumes that its purpose is to be handy in case I wake to the sound of thugs breaking down the door (and foolishly ignoring the loud barks from the other side), or some similar scenario. As home defense scenarios go, this is reasonable, I guess . . . certainly enough of my fellow citizens have had such things happen to them, and arrangements such as these have successfully saved their lives. However, I think going much beyond having a pistol, Surefire flashlight, and cell phone by the bed for this kind of contingency is stretching the limits of credulity, at least for most people. Having a shotgun or two strategically placed around the house, claymore mines on the stairwells, and so on . . . well . . . yes, I've met some people for whom these are actually prudent precautions. Yes, again, these are *very* unusual people. Mas Ayoob said it best once: a lot of people carrying guns don't even know CPR, which is a whole lot more likely to be necessary to save a loved one than a gun will be.

So let's keep our priorities straight. You wanna decrease your chances of dying an ugly, untimely death? Then cut down on the booze and cigarettes—that, *we know*, will have results. 50mm canons under the eaves, well. . . .

All that being said, a person's home *is* his castle. At least that much of common law and common sense is still intact. So, the thought occurs to me last year that someday I may not be able to legally own a handgun, for whatever reason—society is falling apart, Democrats keep getting elected, state legislatures are fickle—whatever. What am I gonna do then? Since long guns will still (presumably) be available to me, that seems like a logical answer. For the street I'd still pretty much be confined to knives and sticks, but believe me—that doesn't mean I'm unarmed. (It does mean that my ability to effectively defend myself against a young, strong aggressor will diminish with age, though.) But for home defense, a long gun will do almost as well—and often better—than a pistol.

OK, so I decided to go with a rifle. Then what? There were a lot of 'em to pick from. If I were a hunter, I'd have worked around one of my existing hunting rifles, I suppose. But I'm not, so I had to start from scratch. Besides, I wanted to come up with the "best" legal pure home defense long gun I could, no compromises—a dedicated gun optimized to the task.

A home-defense rifle should be a short as possible in order to facilitate maneuvering in confined spaces.

One of the things about home defense guns is that you are freed from the constraints of a concealed or even body-carried weapon. The dominant constraint on a home defense long gun, however, is that its length will affect maneuverability considerably. (I even know of SWAT teams that have eschewed the subgun for hi-cap pistols for this very reason.) So as short a rifle as possible seemed prudent. Sixteen inches of barrel length is the legal minimum, so that's that. Next, as light a gun in a reasonable caliber as possible also seemed smart—again for maneuverability.

Pause for a moment. Why do we care about maneuverability? Isn't the standard doctrine that in case of a home intrusion you ensconce yourself in a "safe room" and call the cops? Uh-huh, that's the textbook response. But I just can't make it so overwhelmingly likely to be possible or prudent that it's all I will plan on doing. Life is complicated and full of variables, and I just refuse to give up the option of moving around the house, of moving to my loved ones, of taking the fight to the intruders, or of fighting my way out of the house, if need be. The U.S. military, which spends a gidzillion dollars figuring this kind of stuff out, has come to accept a maxim: *The best-laid plans seldom survive initial contact.* (I think this is what some of those Latin words on certain shoulder patches say.) Amen.

Where were we? Oh, yeah: as light as possible—which is somewhat dependent on caliber. Have to consider caliber sometime, anyway. Here we get into religious debates, of course. My AR-15 is light and small and shoots a very good bullet. From a ballistic and maneuverability standpoint, it's a good home defense gun. But have you ever fired a .223 inside a small building without ear protection? Let me tell you two things. One, even with ear protection, the pressure and noise are unnerving. Two, you won't be wearing ear protection in an emergency (leastways, I'll take that bet). I'd like to be good for more than one shot before I possibly become dithering and useless. So a pistol-caliber bullet out of a carbine might be good. Except that pistol-caliber bullets don't work against people. Hmmm. Wait—the .357 is perhaps the one pistol-caliber bullet that almost everyone will agree does seem to be effective. The .357 out of a 16-inch barrel should cause few partisans on any side of the ballistic debate to consider me underarmed. Why not a higher powered pistol cartridge, like the .44 magnum? Well, I was convinced that the .357 would be a sufficient stopper, and I wanted to hold down noise and muzzle flash to a minimum. Also, I wanted to minimize overpenetration potential, which is significant in a .44 mag fired from a pistol, let alone a rifle. No, the .357 out of a 16-inch barrel seemed to be in the sweet spot of inherent trade-offs.

Which one—that is, which .357 carbine? Well, the fact is that there aren't too many of them out there. Most choices were in a lever gun format, which I feel has a desirable generic manual of arms—i.e., it's instinctive to load, shoot, manipulate, and reload between rounds—for a dedicated home defense gun. With a lever gun you can leave the chamber unloaded and the safety off and make the gun ready by the instinctive action of cycling the lever. Yes, I know modern doctrine often dictates that on a single-action firearm the safety remains on until you are about to shoot. That works fine with 1911-type pistols where the safety can be swept on and off instinctively as you transition from ready to shooting. Unfortunately, few rifle safeties are that easily manipulated, and you have to make a devil of a choice between increased safety and functioning under duress. Leaving the safety off and maintaining good trigger finger discipline is the compromise answer that most professionals I know have arrived at when faced with this sort of choice.

Now, as to which lever-action .357, there are several choices, all of them good from a quality and reliability point of view. However, there are differences between them with regard to what mechanical manipulations are possible before and after the safety is engaged. This becomes important—in my mind *real* important—when you consider what happens just *after* you have used your lever-action carbine in self-defense—God forbid. Consider: You've just shot another human being or two, and they are bleeding out in front of you. You don't do this every day, so you're pretty rattled. The adrenaline is starting to kick in, so you're shaking. The parasymphathetic backlash—the sugar crash from hell—will be coming soon. Your housemates (family, friends, whatever) are in a hysterical panic. You or they may also be hurt—perhaps badly. Hopefully, someone has found the presence of mind to call the police, who are now on their way. *And all this time you are running around with a single-action rifle—chambered, cocked, and unlocked!* This does not sound good to me. I mean, if you "goof" and the gun goes off, there are only the good guys left to be shot (or an intruder that you're holding at gunpoint, and for whose well-being you are now—ironically—responsible). So what I wanted in a home defense rifle was the ability to *easily and simply make the gun safe AFTER it's been shot.* No lowering hammers by hand. No clearing chambers. No manipulating triggers. A nice, simple button

Here the cat represents any necessary use of your hands in an emergency. You need a sling so that you can use your hands!

to push—that's what I wanted!

The gun that met all these criteria was the Marlin 1894CS. This is a well-balanced, light, maneuverable, fast gun with classic lines and an all-round good "feel"— and it's not too expensive, either. But this gun comes from the factory with an 18-inch barrel and rather poor sights, from a home defense perspective. Making the stock 1894 into my ideal home defense gun involved a few modifications. First, the barrel was cut down to 16 inches and recrowned with a "pickup" crown (in which the barrel end is recessed a bit). The action was smoothed to remove the sand that the factory must have left in the gun, and the trigger/sear was polished. Finally, and most importantly, an XS Express Tritium sight was installed on the front of the gun, and an XS ghost-ring sight was installed on the rear of the receiver. This involved some competent gunsmithing and the filling of the factory rear sight slot (which is on the barrel) with a filler block. This sight system is the best there is for fast pickup and speedy shooting, especially in dim light. I won't be attempting 70-yard shots with this gun—7 yards across my living room is more likely. Any sight system will give you excellent accuracy at that distance in daylight. But few were designed with defense in mind, in which case speed and low-light capability are the paramount concerns. The XS setup *was* designed for this application and is best of breed. Finally, if I had been able to find an aftermarket enlarged safety, I'd have had that installed, too—but I don't know of one.

That was the work done to the gun itself. But because this gun was to be used in a different capacity than it was probably designed for, we also had some accessorizing to do. A tactical sling is a must for a defensive gun (as opposed to a field gun). In a home defense scenario, it's simply not feasible to sling your gun over your shoulder to open a door, fetch a child, de-escalate to empty-hand control of a perpetrator, and so on. Therefore, as odd as it looks, a Blackhawk Snap-Shoot Assault Sling was installed on this little gun. Further altering the down-home look of the Marlin is a Surefire 6 series tactical light. I trust I don't have to explain why a bright white light on a defensive long gun is an absolute necessity. Suffice it to say that the Surefire lights are best in class, and only a fool would not have one mounted on a home defense rifle. Finally, an Uncle Mike's butt stock cartridge holder was added. This added significant reserve capacity to my little home defense gun and "cost" nothing—weight-wise, tactically, or even (almost) monetarily. The net result is a sort of lever-action assault rifle—at least in its looks. It looks odd, but it is utterly functional and precisely the gun for the desired application.

One reason I wanted a lever-action rifle for home defense—as opposed to an autoloading carbine—is so that I can use any kind of round in it. Whether I choose to go with a high-powered cartridge or a multiprojectile frangible one, I know that a lever gun will always cycle. I can therefore load my home defense rifle with whatever ammunition I feel best suits my threat level and surroundings.

So if the day ever comes in which I'm denied my constitutional right to own a handgun, I will still have my funny-looking little rifle at home. You may laugh at it now, but remember that the difference between an ugly duckling and a swan is one of perspective.

Chapter 22

SHOOTING WITHOUT SPECTACLES

Many shooters wear glasses to correct their vision. Without these glasses, it's a pretty sure bet that they can't see either their target or their sights or both. Now, when these folks practice, I'll bet they have their glasses on. But really, what are the chances of your having your glasses on when the **** hits? 50/50? Better yet, what are the chances of their staying on during the first second of a violent encounter (remember—most deadly assaults occur *within arm's reach*, and *someone else* initiates them)?

The lesson's clear: you had better be able to shoot (and fight) without corrective lenses—even if you normally wear them!

For those of you who don't yet wear any type of corrective lenses . . . well, it's just a matter of time. You know the old joke: "Getting old sucks . . . but it beats the alternative." From firsthand experience, I can vouch for the veracity of the first part of this statement. Presbyopia is the name given to the condition in which you cannot clearly see near objects; it

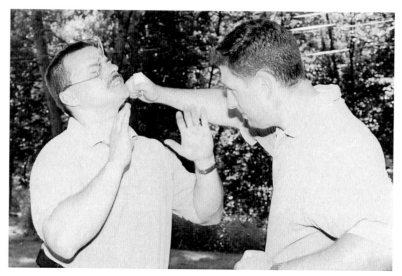
If you wear glasses, assume they'll be knocked off in the opening salvo of a fight.

results from decreased flexibility of the eye lens. Most people over 35 or 40 suffer from presbyopia and therefore have to start using reading glasses. If you're a shooter, you'll probably notice this encroaching condition on the range a couple years before you actually have difficulty reading. It'll go like this (and guess how I know): you'll be shooting in an indoor range, with its typically poor light, bringing your pistol up to eye level, and . . . your sights have vanished! "Damn," you'll mutter, "I could have sworn this gun had sights on it this morning!" This will put you on the horns of a dilemma: you can't use your sights without your reading glasses, but with them, you can't see your target clearly. And besides, you don't have your reading glasses on most of the time anyway, and certainly not in a fight.

So the problem is obvious: many of us need glasses to shoot well, or at least to see either our sights or our target. Yet we can't count on their being available when we might need them most. Is there a solution?

Sighting in Context

Just to set the context, let me restate that most violent assaults occur within five feet, or arm's reach. At these extremely close distances, not only shouldn't you need your sights but you also won't be able to use them anyway because you won't be able to take your eyes off your assailant (and shouldn't even if you could). So at the distances at which you're most likely to have to shoot, you'll be OK. (But—pop quiz here: do you practice point shooting at five feet? You *can* miss even at this close distance, you know—particularly if you don't practice there.) But as you get out to 10 yards or so, you reach a critical distance. This is the realistic maximum distance for almost all defensive handgun shooting, and it's the distance at which even die-hard point shooters agree that using your sights makes sense. So in this chapter, which is concerned with sighted defensive shooting, we'll be talking about shooting from the 10-yard line.

Available Tools

Fortunately, there are sight systems available that can mitigate the problem of not being able to see your sights clearly, and I have experimented with three.

The *XS Big Dot Tritium* sight set. These sights are a modern pistol version of the old Express hunting sights, and, like them, they were designed for fast, close-in shooting. The large white dot that is the front sight is, in the words of Gila-May Hayes, "hard to ignore" and is certainly much easier to pick up than your standard black-on-black post-and-notch sight. I find that I shoot groups about twice as wide with them than I used to with standard black-on-black post-and-notch sights, but others have found that they experience even less group degradation.

The *Crimson Trace* laser. Crimson Trace is the leader in pistol laser sights. Its Lasergrips are plug-and-play replacements for most pistol and revolver grips (the Glock unit requires factory installation). These bright, accurate, rugged laser sights are definitely the first choice in pistol lasers. I must add that there are still many people who dis' lasers . . . and all I can say is that they just don't understand their advantages. Check out Crimson Trace Law Enforcement Training Manager Clyde Caceres' tape *Shots in the Dark* (Paladin Press) to educate yourself.

Tasco's Optima 2000 red-dot sight is a revolutionary sight that was introduced a couple years ago. It's a compact, rugged red-dot sight that's so small it is a thoroughly practical device for a concealed carry gun. Like all red-dot sights, it allows the shooter to maintain target focus while obtaining a sight picture (the 3.5 MOA version was used here).

Finally, the *Heinie Slant Pro* black-on-black, post-and-notch sight set was used as a control in the experiments. One gun was set up with these because they have the deserved reputation of being best in class and are the choice of serious competitive shooters worldwide.

Experimenting with the Sights

I conducted an experiment with each of these four sight systems at the Smith & Wesson Academy with the gracious assistance of then-Director Bert DuVernay. The goal of this experiment was *not* to generate any kind of scientific data—there were too many variables involved for that. Rather, it was to see if there was any consistency between the experiential impressions and anecdotal data generated. The hope is that this experiment will get the ball rolling toward the collection of some wider, more conclusive data. The experiment was conducted as follows:

- Four almost identical S&W 3913-size guns were set up with each of the sights described above. The guns varied very slightly in trigger pull and grip shape.
- Four shooters, each requiring some sort of corrective lenses, participated. Each was allowed 20 minutes to

shoot each gun in any manner he saw fit in order to familiarize himself with the sights.

- From 10 yards, each shooter then shot one string of five rounds in 10 seconds from each gun in two ways: in medium indoor light with glasses and in medium indoor light without glasses.
- The target was a white 18"x24" paper with a black X in the middle.
- Group sizes were recorded by measuring the best four of the five shots.
- Winchester 9mm 124-grain white box ammo was used throughout.

The following shooters took part in the experiment:

- Harry Adams, a well-known Boston-area firearms instructor
- Bert DuVernay, police chief and former director of the S&W Academy
- Bill Porter, retired Michigan State Police lieutenant and an instructor at S&W
- Ralph Mroz, your author

RESULTS AND ANALYSIS

The results of the experiment are presented in Tables 1 and 2. Information about the shooters is in Table 3. The following comments are entirely mine and do not in any way reflect the opinions of the other shooters involved, nor of the Smith & Wesson Academy.

Shooters 2 and 4, who both require reading glasses only, shot better with all four sights with their glasses, the exception being the laser sight, with which sight focus is irrelevant. Shooter 2 shot the optical sights, with which he wasn't familiar, about the same as the two iron sights, with which he was familiar. Shooter 4 shot the Heinie sight, with which he was familiar, best and opened up somewhat on the others.

Shooter 3, who could not see any of the sights but the laser well enough to use them without his glasses, not only shot consistently better without glasses but he also closed his eyes in doing so (for all sights except the laser)! With his glasses, he was affected by the indoor light, and apparently, straining to see his sights caused worse shooting than shooting by feel! Nonetheless, opening his eyes, he did shoot better with the optical sights than with the iron sights, and better with the XS sights than the post-and-notch. Shooter 1 could actually see the sights better without his glasses, but the target became a blur. Apparently, seeing the target more clearly and seeing iron sights less crisply resulted in better shooting, and although we'd expect better shooting when seeing the target better with the optical sights, this wasn't the case—maybe because, as he said, he was affected by the jitter of the dots of these sights.

In fact, all shooters noticed that the laser sight jiggled more on the target than an iron sight seems to (that's because a laser has the full distance to the target—in this case 10 yards—to be affected by hand tremors, rather than the usual 4 inches of barrel length that affects an iron sight (do the trigonometry if you doubt this). This jiggle takes some getting used to. Also, the laser sight demands a full target focus to be effective, and the shooter must learn not to bring his attention back to the gun, which requires unlearning years of training. However, in a real fight chances are you'll be totally focused on the assailant (your target), so the laser sight is more realistic in this regard.

All shooters also noticed that the red-dot sight required the gun to be pretty much in alignment with the target before the dot was easily seen. All valid shooting techniques attempt to instill a "muscle memory" that accomplishes this alignment, but it seems it's a bit easier to correct for large maladjustments with iron sights—I suppose because they are picked up in a wider funnel of vision than a red-dot sight. While this necessity for near-perfect initial gun alignment may seem to imply that out-of-the-holster first-shot speed might be decreased, see how

Table 1

RESULTS OF THE SHOOTING BY SIGHT SYSTEM

	WITHOUT GLASSES Group size in inches	WITH GLASSES Group size in inches
HEINIE		
Shooter 1	5.5	2.5
Shooter 2	4.0	2.5
Shooter 3	3.5	5.0
Shooter 4	2.0	1.5
XS BIG DOT TRITIUM		
Shooter 1	4.0	3.0
Shooter 2	3.5	1.5
Shooter 3	3.0	3.5
Shooter 4	3.0	3.0
TASCO PRO POINT 2000		
Shooter 1	4.5	6.0
Shooter 2	4.0	1.5
Shooter 3	1.5	2.0
Shooter 4	4.5	3.5
CRIMSON TRACE LASER		
Shooter 1	5.0	5.0
Shooter 2	3.0	3.0
Shooter 3	1.0	3.5
Shooter 4	3.0	—

Note: All shooting from 10 yards, medium indoor light, group measures best four of five shots in string.

Table 2
RESULTS OF THE SHOOTING BY SHOOTER

	WITHOUT GLASSES Group size in inches	WITH GLASSES Group size in inches
SHOOTER 1 *Sees sights better without glasses*		
Heinie	5.5	2.5
XS Big Dot Tritium	4.0	3.0
Tasco ProPoint 2000	4.5	6.0
Crimson Trace Laser	5.0	5.0
SHOOTER 2 *Needs reading glasses*		
Heinie	4.0	2.5
XS Big Dot Tritium	3.5	1.5
Tasco ProPoint 2000	4.0	1.5
Crimson Trace Laser	3.0	3.0
SHOOTER 3 *Could not see sights without glasses*		
Heinie	3.5	5.0
XS Big Dot Tritium	3.0	3.5
Tasco ProPoint 2000	1.5	2.0
Crimson Trace Laser	1.0	3.5
SHOOTER 4 *Needs reading glasses*		
Heinie	2.0	1.5
XS Big Dot Tritium	3.0	3.0
Tasco ProPoint 2000	4.5	3.5
Crimson Trace Laser	3.0	—

Note: All shooting from 10 yards, medium indoor light, group measures best four of five shots in string.

Tactical Defensive Training for Real-Life Encounters

Table 3
INFORMATION ABOUT THE SHOOTERS

	EYESIGHT	USUAL GUN	SIGHT FAMILIARITY
SHOOTER 1	Normally wears glasses Saw sights better without glasses	Not the same as used	XS, Heinie
SHOOTER 2	Reading glasses only needed	Same as used	XS, Heinie
SHOOTER 3	Normally wears glasses	Not the same as used	Heinie
SHOOTER 4	Reading glasses only needed	Not the same as used	Heinie

Note: Shooters 3 and 4 are considerably better shots than shooters 1 and 2 with their own guns.

the tentative postulate that follows contradicts this. Also, recall that the fastest, best shots in the world use red-dot sights on their pistols whenever they can.

This small amount of data might seem inclusive at first glance. But remember that this shooting was at 10 yards, where you'd expect reasonably good shots to hold sub-3-inch groups. Remember also that optical sights were completely unfamiliar to all shooters, the XS sights were completely unfamiliar to two shooters (and not the standard sight for a third), and three of four shooters were shooting a different gun (different maker, different grip angle, different trigger system, and different trigger weight) than they were used to (which would account for the somewhat larger than expected groups with the iron sights).

In spite of the seemingly inclusive data viewed in light of these facts, the data does have a bit of a pattern, and I think we can draw the following tentative postulate:

While vision-impaired, most shooters tended to shoot better to only slightly worse with a completely unfamiliar optical sight or XS Big Dot sight. Had they been afforded the same decades of familiarity with these sights as they have been with iron sights, we might then expect them to shoot better with these unconventional sights in circumstances in which they could not clearly see traditional sights.

As to which sight—XS, laser, or red-dot—would come out ahead . . . well, that's unknown as yet and would depend considerably on the application and personal preference anyhow. All are eminently suitable to dim- or even no-light situations. The laser sight has the additional advantage of not requiring the gun to be at eye level to be shot accurately—something that may be vital in a tactical situation.

SUMMARY

I would hope that this little experiment will spur further investigation into the problem of sighted shooting without the spectacles that many of us need to clearly see our sights. It seems that some alternative sight systems—given the same prodigious learning time that traditional iron sights have received—may hold promise.

Finally, thanks very much to the companies who provided equipment and supplies for this experiment: XS Sights, Crimson Trace, Heinie, Tasco, and Winchester. All of these companies are dedicated to saving lives. Thanks also to Bert DuVernay for providing a range.

Chapter 23

THE REVOLVER
AS A SUPERIOR WEAPON

Michael deBethencourt is a contrary man. A well-known knife instructor, he holds his knife "upside down" (tip forward, edge up.) He prefers a stream or foam OC spray, while most instructors incline toward a fog pattern. And even during his tenure as a staff instructor at the Sigarms Academy, he preferred the revolver as a defensive sidearm (and offered a course to that effect there). Now as the director of Northeast Tactical Schools (a university-modeled school with 12 of the Northeast's best-known instructors on staff), he continues to offer his popular Defensive Revolver classes.

Michael usually carries a brace of revolvers in his front pockets (a two-inch Colt Cobra on the right and a two-inch S&W Model 12 [alloy frame] on the left). As a right-hander, his reloads are carried in a speedloader on the right and a Bianchi speed strip on the left because a reload with the left hand is assumed to be one-handed—using the speed strip—and due to an injured right hand. He proffers the most persuasive and extensive number of reasons for the revolver as a superior sidearm that I've encountered, and they are thoroughly convincing even to a longtime slick-slide plastic guy like me. I am now looking at my (Karl Sokol-tuned) K-frame with new appreciation, and I'm looking to build some new ones!

To set the stage, let us remember that for nearly a century (since 1911)—and still in many places—smart, street-savvy pros relied on a revolver as their weapon of choice, and I can't recall any of them ever writing or noting that they felt underarmed as such. The only argument that can possibly be levied against the wheel gun is that it holds but six (or seven or eight) rounds. Well, the standard 1911 holds only eight, and the more compact versions fewer, and none of the .45/1911 bigots (I say that in the nicest way) ever seem to complain that they are underarmed compared to the 15+ round alternatives! And if we are talking about private citizen self-defense (which is what most of us are concerned about), then six rounds should be quite sufficient given that most encounters requiring social gunfire occur at less than five feet. And further, given the short windows of opportunity to survive at these close distances, John Farnam has correctly pointed out that you are more likely to run out of time than run out of rounds. With that in mind, what follows is Michael's list of reasons why the revolver is a superior sidearm.

1) **World's safest live-round indicator.** That is, you do not have to dangerously fiddle with the gun (which is a fair description of a press check) to see if it's loaded. You can see if there are rounds in the cylinder, and if the cylinder is open, you can even feel them in darkness. All this with no unnatural gun manipulation or danger to your body parts.

2) **Requires minimum maintenance.** This is self-explanatory. Revolvers don't require a lot of maintenance. They are easy to clean, and minimum maintenance equals minimum potential for abuse and error while stripping and reassembling.

3) **Offers superior reliability.** Also self-explanatory, this advantage is widely acknowledged. It can't double feed, fail to extract, or fail to cycle. With fewer moving parts and a simpler mechanical operation, you have a weapon with fewer "oops"—or, more likely, "oh s***"—moments. Remember the rule: *Things fail at the worst possible moment.* Also remember that weather extremes will affect a semi's functioning but less so with a revolver.

4) **Faster into action.** Because the cylinder of the revolver causes the grip to sit out just a bit from the body when body-worn, it is easier to grasp in more circumstances than a self-loader that lies right up against your body. Likewise, when lying on a table, the revolver is easier to grasp for the same reason.

5) **Ya seen one, ya seen 'em all.** That is, training on any revolver is training on all revolvers—big or little, large-caliber or small-caliber, and any brand. The manual of arms is the same (or virtually so), and you are instantly familiar with the weapon, even if you've never seen it before.

6) **Fewer shots necessary to prove reliability.** You get a misfunction in a semiauto and it could be anything—the magazine, a spring, the extractor, the ejector, or any of the other dozens of parts—or maybe the ammunition. The gun might work with the next trigger pull or with different ammunition . . . but who knows? With a revolver, if it goes bang the first time, it is 99.9 percent likely to go bang the next five times.

7) **Offers ammunition choice.** A revolver will "feed" and fire any ammunition in the correct caliber. It is not ammunition sensitive, as is a self-loader. Thus you can load to suit your situation. Self-defense loads for the street (possibly variable by season—e.g., frangible for summer, controlled expansion for heavier winter clothing, and so on); game loads for the woods; light loads for training, injured hands/arms, or smaller

shooters; heavier loads and specialty loads for . . . well, you get the idea. Versatile is the word here.

8) **Misfires are reflexively corrected.** Pull the trigger. Which is what you'd do instinctively anyway with any gun under stress. No gymnastics and pidgin English instructions for a lengthy series of refunction maneuvers.

9) **Always available to trusted others.** Everyone knows how to shoot a revolver—point and pull. There's no emergency training time necessary. (*Lessee here, Bobby, this little lever is the decocker—you gonna have to push it down sometimes, and this gizmo is the slide release—which you gonna have to know how to operate. Good luck to ya, 'cause theys a comin' fer us jes about now.*)

10) **Much easier for beginners.** See above.

11) **Loading is easier.** You are loading the gun itself, not a separate appurtenance (the magazine). The loading of the revolver is far more instinctive than that of a semi. Also, you can't load a round in backward; you can't insert a magazine backward.

12) **Easier to unload and make safe.** Two steps vs. whatever.

13) **Easier to shoot.** No double-action/single-action transition, no safeties to manipulate, no hair trigger to worry about, no limp-wrist problems.

14) **Less expensive.** Revolvers are generally less expensive than semis, and many are available in good condition used. This is good in itself, but it also means that you can more easily employ the "fire extinguisher" rule and have guns posted at various spots about your residence, car, or business. This is hardly paranoid, and it has saved the life of several shopkeepers in some well-known incidents. And if you lose one to theft or have to surrender one for evidence, the loss is not as great.

15) **Offers greater tactical versatility.** Deadly-force encounters usually occur at touching distance.

Revolvers can make contact shots (which are instinctive under stress at close distances, and may be necessary in any case) without jamming. Indeed, part of Michael's course stresses contact shots and clever ways to utilize them at close distance.

16) **Safer after the incident.** Responding officers won't accidentally fire your weapon when inspecting or bagging it. It happens. Really.

17) **Looks nicer.** Revolvers are more jury-friendly. They look all-American. They don't look "mean." They don't have hair triggers. They look conservative. John Wayne and all the other Western heroes carried one. Joe Friday carried one. Bad guys in the movies carry death blasters.

18) **Grips are infinitely adjustable.** There are a staggering variety of grips available for revolvers, and you can fit the gun to your hand.

19) **Allows for pocket fire.** With a shrouded hammer (not just bobbed), you can shoot from a pocket. It's damned fast and it's saved lives!

20) **Enables four-season common carry.** A revolver can be carried in the easiest pocket for the strong hand to reach in all four seasons (in a slacks or shorts front pocket in warm weather and a coat outer pocket otherwise). Also, pocket carry is socially acceptable in almost any setting and with almost any clothing style (even in tuxedos, for those formal dinners that so many of us must constantly attend).

21) **Facilitates cheap practice.** You can get .22-caliber revolvers for inexpensive practice, all the while honing your tactics and gun handling.

22) **Points well.** Most people agree that few guns instinctively "point" as well as a good revolver. And if yours doesn't, the pointability can be adjusted with different grips.

23) **Makes stopping power available in a small package.** The small revolvers in .38/.357 caliber are both highly

concealable and deliver potent rounds. There is a reason that the J-frame-size snubbies are the most popular backup and pocket guns in service.

24) **Can't fatally foul the grip.** Get a poor grip on a semiauto, and you can induce a malfunction, activate the magazine release, or fail to depress the grip safety, all of which can deactivate the gun with fatal consequences. With a revolver, a poor grip (which is a distinct possibility during the suboptimal conditions of combat) is still a functional grip.

25) **Less likely to AD.** With a long eight-pound+ trigger (albeit a smooth one), a revolver is much less likely to accidentally or negligently discharge than a single-action semi. No matter how competent you are with your cocked-and-locked 1911, you are a bumbling idiot when roused from sleep, tired, startled, or have a couple beers under your belt.

So there you are: 25 excellent reasons to stick with—or go back to—the wheelgun. A crusty old anachronism? Not hardly!

TEN GOOD TRENDS

I have spent a lot of time on my soapbox these last few years preaching hell and damnation about the current state of affairs in firearms training. I think that the tide may be turning now, so here I thought I'd give you yet another Top Ten list to read—this time about the *good* things that are happening in firearms and firearms training.

1) **The pendulum of individual civil rights swings both ways, and as I write this it is going in the right direction.** With luck, the progress presently being made will stick . . . and accelerate.

2) **Guns have never been better.** Remember when you had to wonder if a new gun was actually reliable? Remember when revolvers were touted as what really serious people carried because reliability was number one? Well, there are still some problems, but modern manufacturing methods and competitive forces have

worked (as Adam Smith has always said they would) to the point that an unreliable new design is now something to call out—not make excuses for. I still don't want to be the first kid on the block to bet my life on a new gun, but we are way improved over where we were 10 years ago.

3) **Virtually every imaginable handgun configuration now exists.** Yes, new designs and firearms are always being introduced, but today you can have virtually any handgun caliber you choose in a gun of your choice of size, weight, and even color. And most of these configurations (although not all) actually make sense given some set of personal preferences and constraints. Now the onus is on us to think through our situation, likely threat, and lifestyle completely and make the optimum choice of weapon.

4) **There is more world-class life-saving training available now than ever.** Two decades ago when I picked up a pistol, there were but three world-class firearms training institutions outside the military. Now there are literally scores. And although some of these are of questionable quality, many—even possibly most—are not. It is a buyer's market. Not to mention that the facilities and training gear (shoot houses, Simunitions, Airsoft, video simulators, etc.) are now superior.

5) **The body of knowledge about warrior science is now vast and increasing.** We know so much more now about what it takes to survive a violent encounter, and even how to teach those skills, than we ever did. The percentage of society that is truly willing and able to fight for the good when necessary has, I assume, not changed. (I'm not talking about professional warriors, i.e., soldiers, but people's character.)

6) **We are in the Golden Age of holster making.** There has never been such an incredible variety of good and competitively priced holsters. I used to say that buying a good gun was easy (just stick to the

major brands and proven models) but that buying a good holster was hard, as there were so few truly good ones out there. That's no longer true.

7) **Handguns are much more effective.** The ammunition, that is, "stopping power," used to be a black art, dependent on the intuition of talented bullet designers, of which there were few. Now every major ammunition manufacturer can design a bullet in any caliber to do whatever you specify it to do in any test medium (within the laws of physics). The result is that there are now many good choices in every caliber for defensive carry.

8) **Accessories and less-lethal weapons are now easy to obtain and effective.** From the "weapon-class" white lights in incredibly small packages to highly effective pepper spray, we no longer have to rely on the gimmick-type intermediate weapons such as the Kubuton, which are, in my opinion, nothing but a sham. Good training for these devices is now also widely available.

9) **Advanced training is now easily available to all.** It used to be that the highly advanced skills of firearms self-defense, Close-Quarters Battle (CQB), and so on were reserved for the Secret Squirrel community. Not everyone needs these skills, of course, but they are a distinct bonus—if not an objective boon—for those who acquire them. And they can be acquired easily at any number of places.

10) **Concern with realism is now getting to be the norm.** Most students now will simply not accept static, outdated, irrelevant survival instruction at advanced levels. Years ago that's almost all there was. Now force-on-force simulations—formally reserved for all but the most advanced classes—are common in almost all classes at some institutions. Fixation with square range drills and their artificial proficiency is giving way to concern with realistic scenario survival.

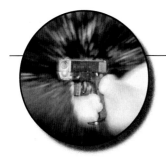

Chapter 25

IT'S OVER

Those of you who've been following the issues in firearms tactics and training over the last decade will by now have noticed something significant. There's been what management theorists call a "sea change" in thinking about how we use handguns in actual encounters and how we train people to survive them. This revolution in thought and approach is now a fait accompli—at least as far as the cognoscenti go.

Now the real work begins—getting this information disseminated and put into action by the legions of trainers and operators everywhere. This is no small task . . . and indeed, not one that's certain to succeed.

What is this sea change in thinking and understanding to which I refer? It is essentially threefold: first, that our central nervous systems undergo significant changes during most life-threatening encounters and that our performance is significantly degraded as a result; second, that the time frames involved in real-life violent encounters are so much shorter than the time frames employed in formulating responses to them that many of those responses are null and void; and third, that practical responses to deadly assaults can only be achieved by realistic force-on-force training.

PERFORMANCE UNDER STRESS

The first principle, the degradation of performance under stress, is a phenomenon that has been well known for a century in scientific circles, and for as long as man has been on this planet otherwise. Soldiers, students of combat, and researchers formulated the fight-or-flight response decades ago and delineated its effects: tunnel vision, threat focus, auditory exclusion, loss of fine motor skill, a distorted sense of time and distance, and so on. This knowledge was pretty much confined to scientific circles and combat war veterans for a long time, however. The great "revolution" in so-called combat shooting that occurred after World War II led us, in fact, in the opposite direction—to technique dependent on sight focus, fine motor skill, and unnatural physical movement. So sexy was its visual result when demonstrated on a nonthreatening range, however, that it took on the trappings and substance of a cult religion. Massad Ayoob was a lone voice in the wilderness in the '70s, trying to refocus us on the reality imposed by our biochemistry and cognitive structure. He called his approach "Stressfire," and it became harder and harder to argue against its factual basis during the '80s and '90s. Then in the '90s a great deal of research and meta-research again led us back to the truth of our fight-or-flight response during the encounters for which we purchase arms and train with them—and this time, the scientific and field evidence was overwhelming.

Today we understand the effects of sympathetic nervous system override, and there is no debate anymore in educated and/or experienced circles about the necessity of basing our training around it. Trainers such as Lou Chiodo in California and Mike Conti of the Massachusetts State Police are now

Massad Ayoob was a pioneer in gunfight performance under stress. His books are timeless and well worth reading.

leading the way in practical, results-orientated training for life-and-death encounters.

The debate is over. The hard work of training begins.

COMPRESSED TIME AND SHORT DISTANCE

The second element mentioned above—that of the extremely short time frames of violent encounters—wouldn't be so important except that most deadly encounters happen at less than five feet! Not five yards, but at nearly touching distance! For far too long, the shooting community has deluded itself into believing that a deadly-force assault should always be met with a deadly-force option—to wit, a firearm. The fact that it is often simply impossible to access and operate a firearm when attacked with focused deadly intent at five feet was entirely glossed over, with some pretty ridiculous techniques passed off for that purpose when pressed. Firearms trainers simply didn't know nongun responses and didn't bother to test their armchair theories at full speed and full force. (My video *Extreme Close-Quarter Shooting*, from Paladin Press, explores this issue in depth.) We're over that now, as far as I can tell, and the educated in the firearms training community now preach the necessity of empty-hand skills for such close encounters.

A true integrated use-of-force approach is now regarded as essential within professional firearms training circles. But the word has yet to get out.

REALISTIC TRAINING

I have written a whole book (*Defensive Shooting for Real-Life Encounters*) on the third principle, the critical importance of realistic training, so I won't dwell on it here. Suffice to say that you can only develop realistic, stress-based, workable responses to deadly-force assaults by practicing them full-speed, full-force, and full-stress against a moving, thinking human being. Airsoft technology and FIST suits make this entirely possible and well within the reach of anyone. There is now a cadre of knowledgeable instructors out there doing exactly this kind of training. If your instructor isn't, you have to ask yourself, "Why?" Answer: Either he (or she) doesn't understand the problem (therefore demonstrating stupidity) or is too embarrassed to put his teachings to a real test (thus admitting incompetence and deceit).

There is no question anymore that realistic force-on-force training is absolutely necessary. Making it happen is the issue.

MEET THE NEW BOSS

Remember the line in The Who's song: "*Meet the new boss, same as the old boss*"? Let's hope it's not the case here. The issues discussed above are now well understood and agreed on by knowledgeable people in the field. But that doesn't mean that that knowledge will wind up in the minds and skill repertoire of the average student. Cultural barriers to change—even demonstrably beneficial change—are often too great for the truth of a new way to overcome. In sports, in business, in health, in relationships, in politics, and in personal development we see everywhere the continuation of old, outdated, dysfunctional, and discredited behaviors. Will that be the case in firearms training? I hope not.

The revolution in handgun training is over—now the real work begins.

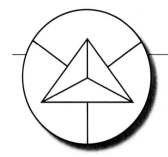

VALIDATING TECHNIQUE THROUGH FORCE-ON-FORCE TRAINING: A BAD IDEA

No one has been a more vocal proponent of force-on-force training over the last several years than I have. I, and many others, have correctly pointed out that static range training is useful for nothing more than developing basic marksmanship and gun handling skills. We have proclaimed to anyone who would listen that force-on-force training with something like Airsoft technology is an absolute necessity for developing the skills that will save a person in a real-life encounter.

And I stand by that last sentence. Force-on-force training *is* a necessity to develop those survival skills.

But too many instructors have made the jump from acknowledging the necessity of force-on-force training to validating their curriculum with it. That is, they point to the fact that the tactics and techniques that they teach hold up well in force-on-force training and conclude that they are therefore validated survival skills.

Wrong, wrong, wrong! They may well be teaching techniques that will get their people killed!

It's wrong because much force-on-force training is different from many real-life encounters. In a spontaneous, violent, real-life fight for your life, you are probably going to drive your sympathetic nervous system into an extreme state that I call SNS override. This state is characterized by the well-known fight-or-flight symptoms: tunnel vision, auditory exclusion, the perceived slowing of time, target focus, and so on. (Note the common misconception that you can't see your sights under this condition. In fact, you can—it's just that you won't because you will be driven to focus instead on the threat, which is actually the tactically sound thing to do at close distances.) In force-on-force training, by contrast, what we are doing is inoculating people to higher and higher levels of stress so that they can perform various weapons/survival techniques *without* suffering the effects of the fight-or-flight (or SNS override) phenomenon.

Notice the difference. In many real-life encounters you will be in the severely debilitated state of SNS override. In force-on-force training, we are training people *not* to enter this undesirable state. *Therefore, we cannot claim that because a technique holds up in force-on-force training that it will be reliable—or even possible—in a real-life encounter.*

We will never be able to determine what works in real-life encounters except through after-action reports and videos of them. In order to respond as if you were in fear for your life, you have to be put in fear for your life—which cannot be done except to actually put your life in danger, and which we obviously cannot do in training. As all Airsoft and Simunitions veterans know, it's the first couple scenarios with these technologies that have any severe stress effect on participants. Participants very soon learn that they won't die and won't even get hurt all that much in them. After these initial scenarios, these simulations do become good validators of tactics and time frames—but they are not forums in which we can observe the effects of genuine fear for one's life, and therefore what works under that condition.

What we hope for in force-on-force training is that the level of stress to which we have inoculated participants will be greater than that which they will experience in a real-life encounter, and therefore that the techniques they have honed in those force-on-force simulations will get them through a real-life situation. This often works as planned when we have control of the real-life situation, such as with warrant executions and hostage-rescue entries. But all too often we see that operators are unable to execute trained skills when they lose control of the situation. In these cases, they simply revert back to whatever Mother Nature allows them to do in the state of SNS override.

So where does this leave us? I submit that for the most part we need to train extensively in those few techniques, tactics, and skills that are possible in SNS override. These basic skills are the only things that will be available to us in most spontaneous encounters (i.e., those not planned by us) and will often be necessary even in those that are. This assumes that we know ahead of time what these skills are. And we do: one-handed shooting, target focus, and so on—the basic curriculum taught by men like Fairbairn and Applegate who'd been there. These skills can be honed successfully with force-on-force training—indeed they need to be. After this baseline of skill has been achieved, we can utilize force-on-force simulations to train more complex skills, by inoculating the operators to high levels of stress. But we need to recognize that unless operators have been trained thoroughly in the basic skills that are possible when their stress threshold has been exceeded, they will be helpless.

Don't be fooled into thinking that force-on-force simulations are verifying that the skills being taught are actually possible under extreme stress. They can't do that.